CLEOPATRA'S PALACE

PALACE

IN SEARCH OF A LEGEND

Discovery
BOOKS

CLEOPATRA'S

In Search of a Legend

PALACE

Discovery
BOOKS

Captions:

Title page: Roland Savoye prepares to film the raising of the statue of a priest of Isis from the seabed of Alexandria's East Harbor.

pp 4–5: Explorer Franck Goddio gazes intently at one of the sphinxes discovered on what was once the royal island of Antirhodos. Its remarkably preserved face is believed to represent Ptolemy XII, father of Cleopatra VII.

pp 6–7: Diver Alain Peton examines hieroglyphs describing a king "endowed with life and power" and inscribed on a red-granite monumental block found on Antirhodos Island. This artifact may have once served as a door jamb in a large, important structure.

pp 8–9: Silhouetted against the waterfront of the modern city, fishermen cast their nets into waters that have for centuries protected the legacy of one of the greatest of ancient cities.

pp 10–11: Diver Eric Smith holds a two-thousand-year-old headless limestone statue of an ibis representing the Egyptian diety Thoth, the god of knowledge and wisdom.

pp 12–13: Divers Jean-Paul Blancan, Nicolas Ponzone, Alaa El Din Mahrous, and Mustapha El Dissouki admire a statue of a priest of Isis and pair of sphinxes, arranged as they may have once appeared at a sanctuary on Antirhodos Island.

pp 14–15: This 1572 engraving by Belgium's Franz Hogenbergh is a Renaissance artist's vision of Alexandria.

pp 18–19: An exotic Cleopatra in Egyptian dress appears in this early 20th-century painting by French Orientalist Alexandre Cabanel.

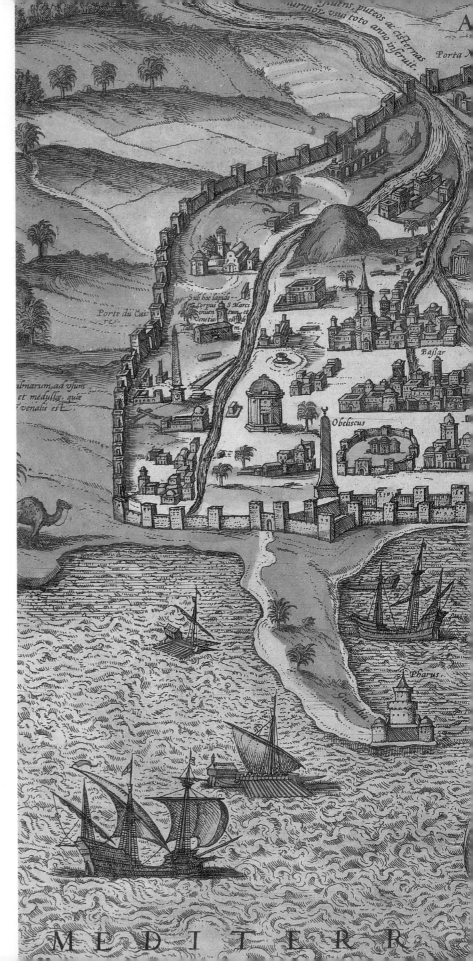

DISCOVERY COMMUNICATIONS, INC.

John S. Hendricks
*Founder, Chairman, and
Chief Executive Officer*

Judith McHale
President and Chief Operating Officer

Michela English
President, Discovery Enterprises Worldwide

DISCOVERY PUBLISHING

Ann-Marie McGowan
Vice President, Publishing

Kathleen Sims
Art Director

Natalie Chapman
Publishing Director

Marcia Foster
Senior Product Manager

Rita Thievon Mullin
Editorial Director

Tracy Fortini
Discovery Channel Retail

Mary Kalamaras
Editor

Discovery Communications, Inc., produces high-quality television programming, interactive media, books, films, and consumer products. Discovery Networks, a division of Discovery Communications, Inc., operates and manages Discovery Channel, TLC, Animal Planet, and Travel Channel.

TEHABI BOOKS

Editorial Development and Book Design
Nancy Cash, *Managing Editor;* Sarah Morgans, *Associate Editor;* Andy Lewis, *Art Director;* Kevin Giontzeneli, *Production Artist;* Maria Medina, *Administrative Assistant;* Tom Lewis, *Editorial and Design Director;* Sam Lewis, *Webmaster;* Tim Connolly, *Sales and Marketing Manager;* Ross Eberman, *Director of Custom Publishing*; Sharon Lewis, *Controller*; Chris Capen, *President*

A CIP catalogue record is available from the British Library.

ISBN 0 297 82554 2

Discovery Communications website address: http://www.discovery.com

Printed in the United States of America on acid-free paper

98765432

First Edition   10 9 8 7 6 5 4 3 2

XA NDR IA.

et spissitudinis ex lapidib. Thebaicis, ut et alij obelisci in ciuitate ... confecta.

Porta del pe...

S Cath arina

Castelle noue

MOSQVE

MOSQVE

Domus Alexandri Magni

Ganophalo.

...ANEVM MARE

CLEOPATRA'S PALACE

In Search of a Legend

Discovery
BOOKS

FOREWORD
by Franck Goddio

For the past three summers, bystanders on the waterfront of the Egyptian city of Alexandria have been treated to an unusual sight. Gazing out to sea, they would have noticed a large white cabin cruiser anchored in the East Harbor—a military zone where civilian vessels rarely go. Looking more closely, they might have glimpsed signs of unusual activity around the ship itself. From time to time, helmeted divers would lower themselves over the sides, while others who had made their way back on board would engage in animated discussions before descending into the water once more.

The divers were my companions, and they were helping me to pursue a quest I had embarked on fifteen years before. It was early in the 1980s that I first heard of the

The hieroglyph above Cleopatra's cartouche reads "Lord of the Two Lands" and would have appropriately applied to Cleopatra, who alone ruled Upper and Lower Egypt.
Left: **Under the waters of Alexandria's East Harbor, Eric Smith examines paving stones that once lined an esplanade on the ancient waterfront of Cape Lochias.**

cataclysms—little reported in the Roman Empire's dying days—that had submerged a large section of the North African littoral, including the original Alexandrian waterfront. That was where Egypt's Greek rulers had chosen to build their homes, so many historic buildings had been submerged beneath the waves.

Although I was busy with other projects at the time, the thought of that sunken shore stuck firmly in my mind. The idea of any drowned city captures the imagination, but by any standards the lost quarter of Alexandria was special. The ghosts haunting its streets included some of the most charismatic figures of antiquity. This was, after all, the city founded and first laid out by Alexander the Great, and the capital of Alexander's successors, the Ptolemies,

Greek-speaking dynasts who endowed it with some of the finest monuments of the classical world.

Above all it was the home of Cleopatra, history's most fascinating woman. It was in Alexandria that she met and mesmerized Julius Caesar, in its now-drowned streets that she, a conqueror of conquerors, caroused with Mark Antony. And it was here that she chose for herself death before dishonor.

More than anything else, it was the drama of Cleopatra's life and loves that drew me to Alexandria and that finally spurred me on in 1992 to undertake the daunting task of locating, mapping, and exploring the remains of the sunken city. H. E. Farouk Hosni, the Egyptian minister of culture, originally encouraged me to pursue my idea. With the generous support of the Supreme Council for Egyptian Antiquities, we have been able to embark on this remarkable task. Now, six years later, much has been achieved—more than I could have hoped when the project was first considered. Whole sunken harbors have been traced, the remains of ancient buildings have been located, and the first reliable plan of the ancient city has been prepared.

Yet if her city has started to yield its secrets, the queen herself has been tantalizingly slow to disclose her own. Just occasionally under the water, while I scrape encrustations from a Ptolemaic column or rest on a pavement where she might have stood, her royal presence suddenly seems near. But now, for the first time, we can see a map of the Royal Quarter as it was before it was submerged, probably around the fourth

From the support vessel *Oceanex*, shown at right moored in Alexandria's East Harbor, Franck Goddio and his team surveyed the seabed for traces of the ancient city, slowly building up an outline of its sunken districts.

***Following spread:* Ceramics from various periods lie scattered along the bottom of the harbor of Antirhodos Island: A diver shines his flashlight on an amphora, possibly North African, from the 2nd or 3rd century A.D.; in the foreground, two Palestinian wine amphorae dating between the 3rd and 4th centuries A.D.; at far right, a large basin from the early Roman period.**

century A.D. To the east, one can see Cape Lochias, on which once stood a royal palace with an inner royal port. Protruding from the ancient ruin-covered sunken coast is a peninsula called the Poseidium on which was built a temple of Poseidon. Antony had a pier built there, on the edge of which he erected a small royal house-sanctuary, the Timonium. It was here that he wished to retire from the world after his defeat at Actium. Nearby several ports housing military and trade vessels testified to the old city's economic strength. In the middle of the Magnus Portus today sits the sunken island of Antirhodos, on which we have discovered architectural remains from several periods as well as building foundations dating back to the third century B.C. We have also excavated a statue and several sphinxes, which most probably were associated with a small temple of Isis. The royal house that Greek geographer Strabo saw on this island had been destroyed by men or earthquakes long before the island was submerged and its ornaments and construction blocks were probably looted and re-used for other constructions. Yet when one visits the site where the royal house once stood, one cannot help thinking that the great queen lived, reigned, and probably died there. Enigmatic yet ever-present, she draws us constantly on toward fresh endeavors. As long as she still has secrets to reveal, my quest continues.

Franck Goddio
Alexandria, 1998

INTRODUCTION

The most famous woman in history is also the most elusive, the most densely shrouded in myth. Written accounts from the times offer only a few glimpses of her, and most of those are through the flawed lenses of her Roman enemies. Ancient historians like Plutarch and Suetonius provide us with only fragments of her story. Less revealing still are history's dusty footnotes: some carvings on temple walls, some cryptic inscriptions, a handful of coins. We know her today not from ancient records, but from later literature and art—from the great writers, especially Shakespeare, who fictionalized her into immortality, and from the artists who, from the Renaissance to the modern era, paid her tribute in the aesthetic idioms of their times.

In most portrayals, Cleopatra is seductively dramatic, a wanton temptress who ensnared men to further her cold ambition and satisfy her perverse appetites. It's a compelling fiction—but hollow.

To get beyond it, we must combine what we know, what we can infer from her time and place in history, and finally, what we can logically imagine. If we do this carefully, we begin to see a very different Cleopatra: a strong, brilliant, visionary woman and, oddly, an uncommonly moral and faithful one. It appears that she loved only two men in her life, and that she was loyal until death, first to one, then the other, even when that fidelity cost her dearly. She lived by her principles with a singular integrity, and ultimately she died by them.

This Cleopatra may not be quite as exotic as the fictional version. But she is just as enchanting, and no less the stuff of legend.

A young and lovely Queen Cleopatra is depicted in this sculpture from the late 1st century B.C. The work was probably a posthumous portrait commissioned by her daughter, Cleopatra Selene, the wife of King Juba of Mauretania.

Chapter I
ROYAL CITY, ROYAL CHILD

A small woman, still lovely despite her grief, she sat holding the wicker basket. She tugged at the basket's lid. It refused to give. She pulled again; she must get it open. Inside were figs, the fat, succulent figs of Egypt. She used to enjoy them so. Inside was also death, and it was death, not figs, that she hungered for now. The lid finally gave way, sliding to the marble floor and rolling away. She stared at the figs, watching with idle fascination as they began to shift, stirred by the snake that lay beneath. Odd, she mused, to want only death, when once she had wanted the whole world—wanted it and almost had it.

Odd too, here at the end, to think only of beginnings, of the history that had created her and the history that she'd lived. She had loved two men—worshiped one, desired the

other. She had borne four children. She had ruled with honor. She had given her noble ancestors no cause for shame. She thought of them, too, her mind drifting far back to the first of them, the golden, gray-eyed warrior with his hands full of grain. . . .

The young soldier-god strode along the shore, his hands filled with ground barley. As he walked, he let the grain drop in thin streams, creating straight, true lines for the city that would rise there. Trudging along in his wake were engineers and architects and soothsayers, none of whom found this exercise unusual. Their leader had already laid out one city, and in his short, matchless career he would found scores of them, naming sixteen after himself: Alexander the Great could never be accused of false modesty.

Legend holds that Cleopatra once impressed dinner guests with her fabulous wealth by dissolving a priceless pearl in wine and drinking it. The story is probably apocryphal; pearls do not dissolve in wine. Nevertheless, it inspired many paintings, among them this early 18th-century work by Anton Schoonyans.

For this particular Alexandria, the conqueror had grand hopes. The site was perfect: a flat and narrow limestone expanse at the edge of the Nile delta, some thirty miles west of the great river's westernmost branch, the Canopic Nile. Nothing stood here now but a little village, Rhakotis. To the south lay a long, coastal lagoon of fresh water, Lake Mareotis. To the north the Mediterranean curved obligingly into the shore to form a perfect deep-water harbor, a magnet for trade, not to mention a superb haven for fighting ships. The land was fertile and the climate incomparable, warmed by the African sun, cooled by the sea winds. The air sparkled.

Egyptian Alexandria would be a gem among cities, and that was fitting, for Egypt was a gem among Alexander's conquests—no less so because the Egyptians had accepted conquest so cheerfully. They had chafed under the Persians, who ousted the last of the native pharaohs in 341 B.C. This Macedonian Greek, sweeping aside the Persians less than a decade later, would surely be an improvement: At least he honored the ancient gods of Egypt, which is more than the Persian governors did.

Alexander stopped in his pacing and looked up to survey his progress, seeing in his mind's eye what did not yet exist, what he would will into being: the broad boulevards, the marketplace, the public gardens, and perhaps a temple to the Greek ruler-god Zeus, or to his Egyptian equivalent, Amon, whose divine son the

The marble head of Alexander the Great, *below,* dating from about 330 B.C., is probably a version of a portrait by his court sculptor Lysippus. *Right:* European-style towers and battlements rise under the direction of Alexander the Great in a highly Eurocentric painting from the *History of Alexander the Great,* written and illustrated by artist Louis Liedet in the 15th century.

Egyptians believed their conqueror to be. And over there, on that slender finger of land stretching into the sea, would be a palace—a whole complex of palaces—where Greeks would wisely rule this age-old kingdom, taking up where three thousand years of pharaohs had left off. He reached into the grain sack and set out again.

A substance called marker white was best for marking terrain, but today none had been available; so, ever inventive, Alexander was using grain from the soldiers' mess. It worked well enough, although he noted that some of it was being lost to the gulls and other birds flocking to feed on it. The soothsayers—always anxious to give their master the most florid version of whatever he wanted to hear—pronounced the birds' coming to be most auspicious, an omen that Alexandria would be prosperous, a great city that fed many strangers.

What the foretellers did not see—or at least did not say—was that Alexander stood today on land that would, in a very few years, become the site of his own tomb. Nor would Greek dominion here last. Three centuries hence, it would end with the death of the only ruler whose legend would ever rival his. She would be his kinswoman, sharing his sister's name: Cleopatra.

PHILIP OF MACEDONIA

Had he not sired a genius even greater than himself, Philip II of Macedonia would be remembered as the preeminent warrior-king of antiquity—one of the greatest generals, in fact, of all time.

When he was born in 382 B.C., however, a glorious future seemed unlikely. Among the constantly warring Greek city-states, Thebes was the ascendant military power and Athens, as always, the cultural heart. Although the Macedonians were, in ways, an accomplished people, to the elite-minded Athenians, they were seen as primitive—a crude, brawling, hard-drinking lot who spoke a Greek so tainted that Athenians could hardly understand it. Yet Philip's gifts were prodigious enough to launch his homeland toward world mastery.

Brilliant, ruthless, and often charming, a superb diplomat and fearless warrior, Philip siezed the throne of Macedonia in 359 B.C. after disposing of several royal relatives. He brought order to his own kingdom and turned its army into the most fearsome in the Aegean. Then he set about uniting all of Greece. Oddly, he seems to have been motivated partly by a sense of inferiority, a yearning for the respect of Athens: Philip's admiration of the Athenians was exceeded only by the contempt with which they returned it.

But even haughty Athens cowered as the Macedonian brought kingdom after kingdom into his camp—by diplomacy if possible, by force if necessary. By 336 B.C., with almost all of Greece (including Athens) united behind him, Philip dreamed of conquering Persia, the most powerful empire on Earth. But it was not to be. In rising to national power, he had neglected his Macedonian base, and he was assassinated by his domestic enemies.

He left behind, however, a son not only worthy of him but destined to eclipse him: Alexander the Great. And in all likelihood, Philip left another legacy: the Ptolemaic dynasty. Although his name is absent from the Ptolemies' genealogical table *(right)*, it is widely believed that during an adolescent dalliance, the sexually precocious Philip sired the child who would become Ptolemy I of Egypt.

Below: **A gold medallion portrait of King Philip II of Macedonia, father of Alexander the Great.**

THE LINE OF THE PTOLEMIES

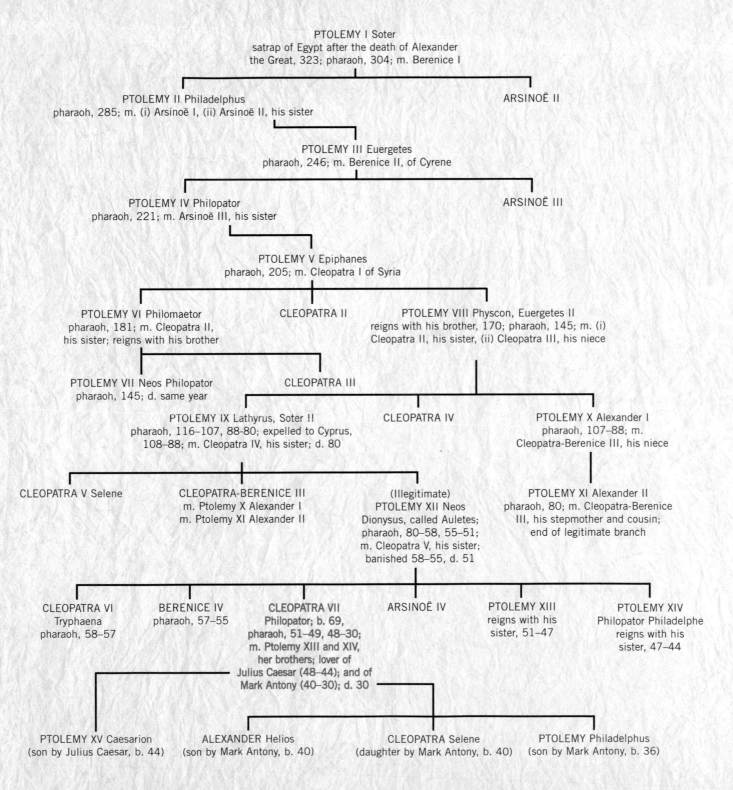

PTOLEMY I Soter
satrap of Egypt after the death of Alexander
the Great, 323; pharaoh, 304; m. Berenice I

PTOLEMY II Philadelphus
pharaoh, 285; m. (i) Arsinoë I, (ii) Arsinoë II, his sister

ARSINOË II

PTOLEMY III Euergetes
pharaoh, 246; m. Berenice II, of Cyrene

ARSINOË III

PTOLEMY IV Philopator
pharaoh, 221; m. Arsinoë III, his sister

PTOLEMY V Epiphanes
pharaoh, 205; m. Cleopatra I of Syria

PTOLEMY VI Philomaetor
pharaoh, 181; m. Cleopatra II,
his sister; reigns with his brother

CLEOPATRA II

PTOLEMY VIII Physcon, Euergetes II
reigns with his brother, 170; pharaoh, 145; m. (i)
Cleopatra II, his sister, (ii) Cleopatra III, his niece

PTOLEMY VII Neos Philopator
pharaoh, 145; d. same year

CLEOPATRA III

PTOLEMY IX Lathyrus, Soter II
pharaoh, 116–107, 88-80; expelled to Cyprus,
108–88; m. Cleopatra IV, his sister; d. 80

CLEOPATRA IV

PTOLEMY X Alexander I
pharaoh, 107–88; m.
Cleopatra-Berenice III, his niece

CLEOPATRA V Selene

CLEOPATRA-BERENICE III
m. Ptolemy X Alexander I
m. Ptolemy XI Alexander II

(Illegitimate)
PTOLEMY XII Neos
Dionysus, called Auletes;
pharaoh, 80-58, 55–51;
m. Cleopatra V, his sister;
banished 58–55, d. 51

PTOLEMY XI Alexander II
pharaoh, 80; m. Cleopatra-Berenice
III, his stepmother and cousin;
end of legitimate branch

CLEOPATRA VI
Tryphaena
pharaoh, 58–57

BERENICE IV
pharaoh, 57–55

CLEOPATRA VII
Philopator; b. 69,
pharaoh, 51–49, 48–30;
m. Ptolemy XIII and XIV,
her brothers; lover of
Julius Caesar (48–44); and of
Mark Antony (40–30); d. 30

ARSINOË IV

PTOLEMY XIII
reigns with his
sister, 51–47

PTOLEMY XIV
Philopator Philadelphe
reigns with his
sister, 47–44

PTOLEMY XV Caesarion
(son by Julius Caesar, b. 44)

ALEXANDER Helios
(son by Mark Antony, b. 40)

CLEOPATRA Selene
(daughter by Mark Antony, b. 40)

PTOLEMY Philadelphus
(son by Mark Antony, b. 36)

(Adapted from E. Flamarion, *Cleopatra: The Life and Death of a Pharaoh*,
based on E. M. Forster, *Alexandria: A History and a Guide*; all dates are B.C.)

ALEXANDER THE GREAT

If ever a man was born for conquest, it was Alexander of Macedonia. From his father, King Philip II, he inherited brilliance, a genius for warfare, a superb army, boundless ambition, and a nation united under one rule. From his mother, Olympias, a princess of Epirus, came his magnetic physical beauty and his unshakable faith in his own destiny: Olympias, who had come to hate her philandering husband, assured her young son that his father was not Philip but Zeus, king of the gods.

Olympias' family claimed descent from Achilles, and this peerless Greek warrior of legend was Alexander's paradigm: Throughout his life, he slept with a copy of Homer's *Iliad* under his pillow. He, like Achilles, would seek glory above all things.

Alexander's military training, harsh and continuous, began when he was a child. By the age of sixteen he was leading troops into battle, and by eighteen he was his father's finest general. The relationship between father and son was a murky brew of mutual pride and jealousy, but they were closest during the military campaigns they shared.

Learning from Philip, Alexander became a master strategist and tactician and a wizard at deploying an army whose spine was an infantry armed with *sarissas,* wooden pikes nearly twenty feet long which turned a Macedonian phalanx into a bristling, unstoppable tank. Philip was concerned that his son know how to rule as well as conquer, however, so he procured for him the best tutors, chief among them the great philosopher Aristotle.

Alexander was only twenty when his father was assassinated, but he was uniquely prepared to lead. He put down revolts in Thrace and

Thebes, then turned toward achieving what Philip had not lived to do: the conquest of Persia. With only thirty thousand infantry and five thousand cavalry, he set out on this colossal venture in 334 B.C.

The first major battle after the army crossed into Asia Minor came at the river Granicus. Riding at the head of his cavalry, Alexander mounted a charge so furious that the Persians fled in terror. He then marched down the Ionian coast, liberating one Greek city after another from Persian rule. At the town of Issus, on the coastal plain north of Syria, his army of thirty-five

thousand won one of the greatest tactical victories in military history, routing a Persian host of three hundred thousand men.

Alexander went on to conquer the city-state of Tyre, marching from there through Palestine and into Egypt, the last of Persia's Mediterranean lands, which welcomed him as a liberator. His stay was short but fateful. He founded Alexandria, and at Memphis he was hailed as pharaoh, inaugurating Greek rule in Egypt. The most personally significant event in Egypt, however, must have been his long and difficult desert trek to the Siwa oasis shrine of Amon, the Egyptian analog of Zeus. There the priest hailed him as the god's son, confirming the story of divine birth Olympias had told him as a child.

Like Achilles, Alexander would die young—but not before amassing a personal empire unequaled before or since, and fulfilling the destiny he had never doubted: becoming the greatest conqueror the world had ever seen.

Left: A 16th-century French illustration shows Alexander being lowered to the seabed in a glass cage so fishes can pay him homage.

Like most visitors, Alexander found Egypt mysterious, alluring, enchanting. Even so, he stayed for less than a year. He had pressing business in the east. He would go on to complete his conquest of the vast Persian empire and other lands beyond, sweeping into Media and Scythia and finally into India, where he believed the world ended on the shores of an all-encompassing sea.

But if the sea was there, he never saw it. The tally of hardships he and his men endured began to rival the tally of victories, and his war-weary troops finally persuaded him that they had been away from home long enough. Reluctantly he turned, leading a torturous march back to his new capital, Babylon. And there two years later, in 323 B.C., he met his fate, felled not by another general—none had ever defeated him—but by a tiny natural foe: a mosquito perhaps, or a microbe. He was inspecting a drainage project in the swamps along the Euphrates River when he contracted a fever that his battle-ravaged body couldn't repel.

A general at sixteen, king at twenty, ruler of most of the known world before he was thirty, Alexander the Great was dead at thirty-three. He had amassed an empire that sprawled over three continents, stretching from Greece down to northern Africa, to Asia Minor and across western Asia to the Indian subcontinent. No one man had ever conquered so much territory; no man ever would again.

The world he left was very different from the one he had entered. Alexander's march had pulled behind it a tidal surge of Greeks—soldiers, traders, settlers, and bureaucrats who brought with them Greek customs, gods, art, and learning to mingle with the native cultures that came under his writ. The resulting Graeco-Asiatic mix, called Hellenism, gave its name to an age that was the most cosmopolitan ever known, and one of the richest. Alexander had put captured Persian treasure into circulation, and more money meant new vigor in trade and commerce and building—new cities, roads, waterways, new arteries between West and East. Even as his empire grew, he made the world smaller.

He had also been wise enough to know that immense territories couldn't be ruled without the cooperation of the conquered, and that meant respecting their ways and co-opting their governmental structures. These things he usually did, so that by the time he died he left behind a state of uncommon unity, a world enjoying a rare degree of peace—however temporary.

The passing of such a man required a fitting funeral, and two years went into preparing it. Not until 321 B.C. did the funeral cortege set out, bearing Alexander from Babylon toward the bleak mountains of his native Macedonia and internment at the hill fort of Aegae—by ancient custom the burial ground of Macedonian kings. During the journey, his body, preserved in precious spices, lay in a coffin of beaten gold, overspread with gold-embroidered purple cloth. Above it, riding on a wagon with gilded wheels, rose a gold temple, its vaulted roof studded with jewels and topped by a gold olive wreath. Mounted at each corner was a statue of Nike, goddess of victory. Under a golden cornice below the roof hung a painted frieze, its four panels depicting Alexander's greatness in battle: the general in his chariot, his war elephants, his ships, his cavalry. The wagon and its burden were drawn by sixty-four mules pulling four abreast, each adorned with a jeweled collar and a golden crown with dangling bells.

Months of travel took the procession north along the Euphrates, then east to the Tigris before it edged along the northern border of the Arabian Desert. There it was met by one of Alexander's faithful generals, Ptolemy, who at the time was de facto governor of Egypt.

Eleven years older than Alexander, Ptolemy had known the conqueror almost from birth. They were distant kin on Ptolemy's maternal side, but there was very likely a tighter tie of blood than that: Common report said that Alexander's father, King Philip of Macedonia, was also Ptolemy's real father, making Ptolemy and Alexander half-brothers. Certainly they were close. Ptolemy had been by Alexander's side throughout the conqueror's meteoric career, part of his trusted inner circle. Now, leading an army, the general purportedly approached to do homage to the fallen hero.

In fact, he was there to hijack him. Ptolemy and his men attacked the funeral train, stole the body in its shining shrine, and fled with it back toward Egypt, intending to install it in the city the conqueror had founded. Alexander's remains would be a talisman,

Ptolemy knew—a sacred relic legitimizing the general's own dynastic plans.

Down past Tyre and through Judea went Ptolemy's army with its precious cargo, bearing it first to the former Egyptian capital of Memphis at the head of the Nile delta, there to wait in its golden car for several years while a tomb was built in Alexandria. In the new capital, the soldier-god would finally come to rest, lying in splendor over the years as the mausoleums of the Ptolemies sprang up around him. And just as the first Ptolemy had hoped, his boyhood friend and half-brother seemed to bring good fortune with him, even in death: Of all the conqueror's inheritors, the Ptolemies would last the longest and fare the best.

As Alexander had lain dying in Babylon, the question of succession had been put to him. Who would rule his empire now? At length he mustered enough strength to whisper "the strongest."

Legend has it that Eris, the grim Greek goddess of discord, once disrupted a feast on Olympus by tossing onto the banquet table a golden apple inscribed "for the fairest." Predictably, all the goddesses claimed it, touching off a dire chain of events that ended on earth with the Trojan War. Alexander's whispered prediction about "the strongest" had much the same effect. Several of his generals thought themselves fit heirs to the empire, and the conqueror's corpse was scarcely cold before the in-fighting began. It would go on for years.

Finally, it sorted itself out: A general named Antigonus would rule Macedonia, the homeland, and much of Asia Minor. His fellow-officer Seleucus would take a sprawling domain that included Syria, Mesopotamia, and Persia; and Ptolemy would have Egypt.

But fissuring of the empire continued. Greece devolved into petty, warring city-states; Antigonus had lost significant holdings to Cassander and Lysimachus. A tribe called the Parthians on the Iranian plateau began hacking away at the Seleucids' east and center, and at the

A limestone temple relief from Luxor shows the hieroglyphic titles of Alexander the Great: King of Upper and Lower Egypt and Lord of the Two Lands. These were the titles usually accorded a pharaoh of Egypt. *Right:* A marble rendering of Ptolemy I Soter, founder of the Ptolemaic dynasty.

same time, the Ptolemies grabbed some of their western holdings. Boundaries softened and shifted. And as the heirs of Alexander and their sons and grandsons fought and bickered, bought, traded, bargained, betrayed, plotted, and killed, a formidable new power rose in the west: Rome. By the early second century B.C., the Romans had become a thorn in the side of the Hellenistic monarchs. In the rich kingdom of Egypt, the Ptolemies felt as discomfited as the rest.

Rather unimaginatively, all the kings of the Ptolemaic line had the same name—Ptolemy—so they all adopted additional descriptive names that set them apart. Ptolemy I, formerly Alexander's general, was called Soter, meaning "Savior." He did prove to be a capable leader, far more respected than the Persian governors ousted by Alexander. During his reign and that of the two Ptolemies who followed, Egypt was the most stable and prosperous of the Hellenistic kingdoms. The Macedonian overlords declined to tamper much with existing Egyptian institutions and bureaucratic structures; they even grafted some significant native practices onto their own Greek heritage.

KINGDOM OF CASSANDER

KINGDOM OF LYSIMACHUS

THRACE

Black Sea

BITHYNIA

PONTUS

MACEDONIA

Aegean Sea

CYZICUS

GORDIUM

ANCYRA

PERGAMUM

SARDIS

IPSUS

KINGDOM OF ANTIGONUS

ARMENIA

DELPHI

EPHESUS

ZEUGMA

THEBES

MILETUS

CORINTH

ATHENS

(GREECE)

SPARTA

TARSUS

ANTIOCH

NINEVEH

SYRIA

CRETE

CYPRUS

DURA

GEBAL

PALMYRA

Mediterranean Sea

SIDON

DAMASCUS

Tigris

Euphrates

TYRE

BABYLON

CYRENAICA

JERUSALEM

GAZA

ALEXANDRIA

PELUSIUM

KINGDOM OF PTOLEMY

MEMPHIS

Nile

(EGYPT)

Red Sea

PTOLEMAIS

THEBES

After the death of Alexander the Great in 323 B.C., his empire was divided among three of his generals: Egypt went to Ptolemy, Alexander's lifelong friend, biographer, and most likely his half-brother; Greece to Antigonus; and vast territories east of Egypt to Seleucus. The three men were the founders, respectively, of the Ptolemaic, Antigonid, and Seleucid dynasties. By 303 B.C. it was clear that of the three, Ptolemy was by far the most successful. His dynasty would last for three centuries. Antigonus would lose a significant portion of his land to Cassander and Lysimachus, while the Seleucids would steadily lose ground to the Ptolemies and to the fierce Parthian warriors of the Persian plateau.

N

0   400km

0   250mi

The Divided Empire, 303 B.C.

Alexander's Empire

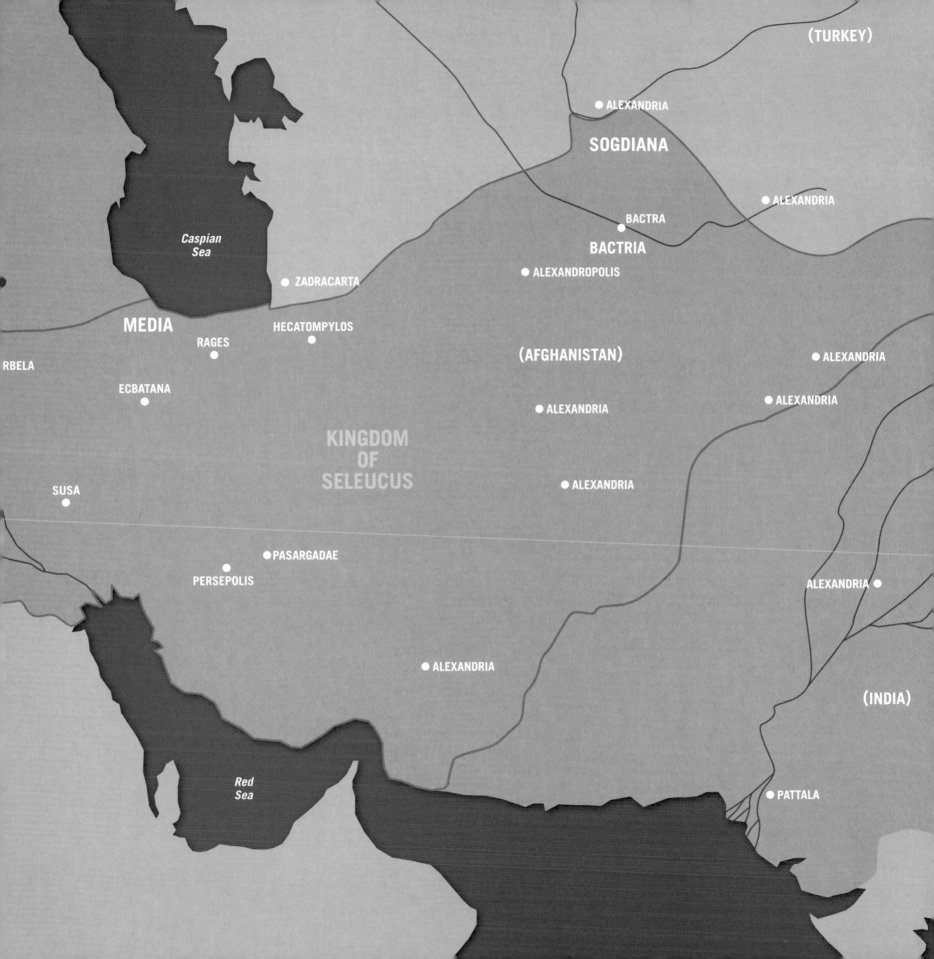

For one thing, they assumed the notion of divine, hereditary kingship, the ruler being associated with Amon or with Horus—son of the great mother-goddess Isis and her brother/husband Osiris, Lord of the Dead. In addition, they adopted the practice of royal incest, the marriage of brother and sister—god appropriately wedded to goddess. This scandalized other Greeks, and it appalled Rome, but it had the practical advantage of limiting disputes over succession—to some extent, anyway.

Despite ties of blood and marriage, Ptolemaic family members killed each other off from time to time in their pursuit of power, a habit that was at least as much Macedonian as Egyptian. (Alexander's own father, the crafty and brilliant Philip, had himself dispatched two half-brothers on his way to the throne of Macedonia.)

But the worst of the familial rivalries came later in the dynasty. The early Ptolemies prospered in Egypt, growing ever richer and expanding their territorial boundaries. Ptolemy I conquered Cyrenaica to the west of Egypt, occupied southern Syria to the east, took Cyprus and several islands in the Aegean, and even put garrisons on the Greek mainland. To the north, his influence extended through Asia Minor and across the Bosphorus to the shores of the Black Sea. A builder as well as a conqueror, Ptolemy I also oversaw the first stages of Alexandria's rise to architectural and cultural splendor.

Having secured his place in history and enlarged the realm he would leave to his favorite son, he died peacefully in his bed—a rare thing for a general or a Ptolemy—at the age of eighty-four in 285 B.C. Ptolemy II Philadelphus ("He Who Loves His Sister") continued his father's policy of territorial expansion, and his son, Ptolemy III Euergetes ("Benefactor") took the policy to its zenith in the middle of the third century B.C., occupying all of

An eight-drachma gold piece, *below*, minted in Alexandria in the 3rd century B.C. shows the profiles of Ptolemy I of Egypt *(left)* and his queen, Berenice I.

Syria to the very banks of the Euphrates and conquering Babylonia and Persia.

But the kings who followed pitched the dynasty into steep decline. Ptolemy IV was a monster who murdered his own mother, not to mention a brother and an uncle. Ptolemy V, whose reign began in 205 B.C., lost all of Egypt's foreign possessions except Cyprus. And Ptolemy VIII, who ruled with his brother Ptolemy VI for a time before assuming the kingship alone in 145 B.C., was probably the most bizarre and bloody of the entire line. Nicknamed Physcon ("Fatty"), he was so enormous that whenever he sat down, servants had to hoist him to his feet to make him mobile again. His bottomless appetite for food was apparently matched by his appetite for gore: He killed his own son, dismembered the body, and sent pieces of it to the boy's mother as a birthday present.

Physcon was the bloated emblem of how thin the Ptolemaic blood was running and how vulnerable Egypt was becoming to outside meddling. But even before his time, the specter of Rome was looming ever larger. During the reign of Ptolemy VI, when Egypt found itself losing a war with neighboring Syria, only the intervention of a Roman legate preserved Ptolemaic rule. Thereafter, Rome and Egypt were inextricably linked.

It was never an easy relationship, for the Romans and the Hellenistic Egyptians were fundamentally different. Romans were conservative to the core, holding to the principle of *mos maiorum,* fidelity to the ways of one's ancestors. They valued—or said they valued—simplicity, frugality, and moral rectitude. They honored Classical Greece (indeed, they showed their admiration by stealing or slavishly imitating the best of its art). But Hellenistic Greeks were another matter. Romans considered them degenerate, sly, devious, ostentatious, licentious, and excessive in every way.

THE MAGICAL GODDESS

Isis was the daughter of the earth god Geb and the sky goddess Nut, and she was married to her brother Osiris. Together they were the benefactors of humankind, giving the world agriculture, law, and civilization itself. All people loved them, a fact that elicited the envy and hatred of their brother Seth, Lord of Evil. Seth killed Osiris by sealing him into a chest and casting it adrift on the Nile to float out to sea. Isis eventually found her husband's body and brought it home to Egypt, only to have Seth rend it into fourteen pieces and throw them into the Nile for crocodiles and fishes to eat. Impelled by her devotion, however, Isis searched out thirteen of the pieces and magically restored Osiris' body. Thereafter he became the Lord of the Dead.

For her efforts on his behalf and her care of their child, the falcon-headed sky god Horus, the goddess became widely venerated as the ideal of the loving wife and mother, admired for her creativity and compassion. The embodiment of feminine virtue, she was nevertheless no passive paradigm: Isis was the mistress of powerful magic, a goddess who could bend even fate to her will.

According to myth, Isis and Osiris once lived on earth and ruled Egypt, and thus both were closely associated with royalty. Indeed, the hieroglyph representing her name resembled the throne to which the pharaohs were said to have been born. As a symbol of passion linked to sovereign power, Isis must have held strong personal appeal for Cleopatra, her avatar on earth.

These bronze statuettes of Isis, *left,* and Osiris, *right,* probably date from the Ptolemaic period. Osiris is shown in mummiform, his body shrouded, indicating his role as Lord of the Dead. The Isis figure was originally suckling the infant god Horus, which apparently was broken off from the rest of the sculpture. Her crown contains a solar disk enclosed in the cow horns of Hathor, goddess of love and joy, with whom Isis was sometimes associated.

The Ptolemies were excessive, without apology. They found nothing immoral in lavish display; rather, they felt that reveling in their wealth was the least they could do to thank the gods for the gift of it. There was even a Greek word for this sort of luxuriousness: *tryphe*. As for the Romans, the Hellenistic Egyptians thought them drab, moralizing hypocrites and cruel, rapacious, semi-civilized upstarts.

Still, there was no separating the fates of Rome and Egypt. Rome prized Egypt's wealth and had grown addicted to its grain. For their part, the Ptolemies had come to count on Rome's power to prop up their enfeebled dynasty.

The later Ptolemies had to walk a precarious tightrope, taking care not to offend the Romans while at the same time maintaining some semblance of independence. A misstep on either side invited the wrath of Rome on one hand, the contempt of their own people on the other. That was the state of things in the first century B.C., the time of Ptolemy XII Auletes ("The Flute Player"), father of Cleopatra, the seventh Ptolemaic princess of that name.

By the time Auletes took the throne in 80 B.C., it was clear that whatever the designs of Rome or the imperial fortunes of Egypt, Alexander's soothsayers had been right about the prospects of Alexandria: It had grown into a great city that fed many strangers. It was, in fact, the largest, richest, most splendid city on earth. Compared with its magnificence, Rome was little more than an overcrowded, evil-smelling slum.

More than half a million people of all races and religions inhabited Alexandria, the crossroads of

A wall painting from a noble's tomb at Thebes shows Egyptian peasants threshing grain. The tomb dates from the 18th Dynasty, which ruled from 1570 to 1293 B.C., so this depiction of Egypt's agricultural wealth was already ancient in Cleopatra's day.
Below: These faience vessels date from the Ptolemaic period. At left is a New Year's flask, used in rituals to celebrate the annual flooding of the Nile in July. The baboon figures on the neck represent the god Thoth as the Reckoner of Time. At right is a Roman cup.

Europe, Africa, and Asia. Three groups predominated: The Greek upper class lived in the center of the city; the Jews, who formed the core of the merchant class, were concentrated in the eastern quarter; and the native Egyptians occupied the western quarter. These citizens shared the city's wide, limestone thoroughfares with many visitors, for Alexandria was the hub of caravan routes stretching from Africa eastward to China and India and sea routes spanning the Mediterranean littoral.

Rome could not begin to match the volume and variety of goods flowing in and out of Alexandria's great port. The most important export was wheat, nurtured by the Nile mud and destined to feed other Mediterranean lands, but cargo ships carried much else besides: African ivory and ebony, emeralds and amethysts, chased silver plate, exquisite decorative glassware, wool and linen, cinnamon and other rare spices, fruits and wines, alluring scents, and the papyrus that was the writing paper of scribes and scholars everywhere.

Beacon to the World

The famous lighthouse at Alexandria was the only one of the Seven Wonders of the Ancient World that had a practical, secular use. Its architect Sostratus—a contemporary of the Greek mathematician Euclid, who lived at Alexandria—most likely designed this elegant and scientifically useful structure, employing the principles of Euclidian geometry. Commissioned by Ptolemy I, the lighthouse was completed during the reign of his son, Ptolemy Philadelphus. The island on which it was built was known as Pharos, a variation of "Pharaoh's island," according to some ancient beliefs.

The tallest building of its time, the lighthouse towered more than 423 feet above the harbor, its beacon visible to sailors more than thirty miles offshore. Greek traveler Strabo, who visited Alexandria in A.D. 27, described the hazardous harbor: *"Pharos is an oblong isle, is very close to the mainland and forms with it a harbour with two mouths, for the shore of the mainland forms a bay, since it thrusts two promontories into the open sea, and between these is situated the island, which closes the bay, for it lies lengthwise parallel to the shore. Of the extremities of Pharos, the eastern one lies closer to the mainland and to the promontory opposite it (the promontory called Lochias), and thus makes the harbour narrow at the mouth; and in addition to the narrowness of the intervening passage there are also rocks, some under the water, and others projecting out of it, which at all hours roughen the waves that strike them from the open sea. And likewise the extremity of the isle is a rock, which is washed all round by the sea and has upon it a tower that is admirably constructed of white marble with many stories and bears the same name as the island. This was an offering made by Sostratus of Cnidus, a friend of the kings, for the safety of mariners . . . for since the coast was harbourless and low on either side, and also had reefs and shallows, those who were sailing from the open sea thither needed some lofty and conspicuous sign to enable them, to direct their course aright to the entrance of the harbour."*

For centuries the remarkable tower guided ships safely into the Great Harbor, with the bright glow emanating from the fire burning at its top, its light directed by an immense, polished-bronze mirror.

Built to endure time, the lighthouse continued to be the steadfast beacon for centuries, weathering the region's many storms and earthquakes. Finally, however, it suffered significant damage from a series of powerful earthquakes, the worst of which occurred in A.D. 1308. By A.D. 1349, it was so badly compromised that it could no longer function. When the Arab traveler Ibn Battuta visited the city in that year the lighthouse was so seriously undermined that he could not even climb up to its doorway.

Left: **This reconstruction of what Alexandria's famous Pharos lighthouse may have looked like is a little misleading. According to ancient sources, the structure had only three levels: a square base, an octagonal second tier, and a round tower at the summit that held the powerful beacon fire.**

As a maritime facility, the port had no equal. It was protected from the open sea and north winds by reefs and the three-mile-long island of Pharos, which lay three-quarters of a mile offshore and was connected to the mainland by a breakwater, the Heptastadium. The Heptastadium divided the port in two. On the eastern side was the Great Harbor, protected by artificial breakwaters. The man-made Harbor of Good Return lay to the west. Each harbor could hold twelve hundred ships at a time. Vessels were guided in and out of port by one of the Seven Wonders of the World, the Pharos lighthouse.

Built under Ptolemy II by the architect Sostratus, the elegant, white-marble lighthouse towered 423 feet above Pharos island. It was constructed in three successively smaller tiers, the first square in shape, the second octagonal, and the topmost one round and surmounted by a huge statue of Zeus. Within the round tier a fire burned day and night, magnified by a polished bronze mirror that slid along in a groove around the perimeter of the flames to direct the light. The beacon was visible to ships thirty miles away.

The lighthouse was Alexandria's proudest engineering achievement, but the city boasted many other construction marvels. A complex of canals, reservoirs, and filters purified the waters of Lake Mareotis and the Nile, providing fresh water in abundance. Another canal joined the lake to the river, and it was said that the volume of river trade between Alexandria and the rest of Egypt actually surpassed the volume passing through the port.

Visitors, even those accustomed to the splendors of the Far East, were invariably struck by the beauty of Alexandria. They gaped at its imposing monuments of marble, red granite, and limestone, at its many temples and theaters and amphitheaters. A particularly awe-inspiring attraction was the Serapeion—the temple of Serapis, Hellenistic in style and with a golden roof. It was originally erected to honor a syncretic god introduced to Egypt by the Ptolemies and com-

This Egyptian-style bronze statuette of a striding king dates from the Ptolemaic period. The king's extended hand once held a staff of office, and he wears the double crown of Upper and Lower Egypt, adorned in front by a cobra symbolizing royalty.

bining attributes of the Egyptian deities Osiris and Apis and Greece's Zeus and Aesculapius. Later, it was rededicated to learning and became an annex to the most famed of all Alexandria's attractions: the magnificent Library and Museum. These great edifices, built in the Royal Quarter by the first Ptolemy, were compelling both as structures and as symbols, signifying that Alexandria was not only the commercial center of the world but also its cultural heart.

The Library of Alexandria was the place where human scholarship and science came of age, the place where knowledge was first collected and systematized. It was here that Eratosthenes measured—accurately—the circumference of the Earth, that Euclid formulated geometry, that Hipparchus mapped the constellations and assessed the brightness of stars, that Heron invented steam engines and gear trains, that Herophilus identified the brain rather than the heart as the site of intelligence, that Dionysius of Thrace brought form and logic to the study of language, that Archimedes devised mechanical wonders which, once lost, would not be reimagined until the Renaissance. The seven hundred thousand scrolls that lay neatly organized and catalogued on the Library's shelves included the complete works of Homer and Hesiod, and all the plays of Aeschylus, Sophocles, Euripides, Aristophanes, and Menander.

The Museum—literally, a temple to the nine Muses, Greek goddesses associated with the arts and sciences—was also a center of scientific and artistic pursuits. Scholars met there, strolled its breeze-kissed arcades, enjoyed the fine fare of its dining room, and gathered in its great hall to exchange ideas. Like the Library, the Museum had its experts in philosophy, rhetoric, philology, astronomy, geometry, geography, hydrostatics, anatomy, and medicine. So they would not have to waste their intellects on mundane matters, these scholars received royal subsidies: The Ptolemies, for all their faults, treasured and fostered learning.

Jean-Claude Roubaud holds a small jar found at the site of an ancient shipwreck buried in what was the royal harbor of Antirhodos. Like many of the objects found nearby, it more than likely dates from the 1st century A.D.

Right: These two vessels were discovered in the small harbor of Antirhodos Island. In the foreground is a jug from the 1st century A.D. Behind it is a small Egyptian cooking pot that dates between the 1st and 2nd centuries A.D.

The Library: Alexandria's Pride and Tragedy

From the beginning, the Ptolemies spared no effort to ensure that the Library of Alexandria was the greatest monument to knowledge in the world. When Ptolemy I, (Soter), assumed power after Alexander the Great's death, he wanted to create an institution that would rival Aristotle's Lyceum and Plato's Academy. Alexandria, the hub of international trade and cultural exchange, was the perfect environment and attracted scholars and artists from throughout the world, who both sought out and contributed to what would become the unprecedented center of learning.

Following Ptolemy I's death, subsequent rulers continued to build upon his legacy, enriching the Library's increasingly vast archives with the greatest works of art, science, and literature. For some, however, methods of acquiring precious manuscripts were not always honorable ones. Soter's grandson, Ptolemy III, for example, siezed cargoes of books from ships docked at Alexandria and had copies made, which he would return instead of the originals, thus the

term "ship libraries" for works housed in the collection. For the forfeit of a large security deposit, he also "acquired" the original works of Athen's greatest playwrights.

Chicanery and simple diligence paid off. By Cleopatra's reign, the Library's scrolls—perhaps as many as seven hundred thousand—represented ten times the number of books to be found in all of Europe before the invention of movable type nearly fifteen hundred years later. Its only challenger was a grand library in the wealthy city of Pergamum in Asia Minor, but Mark Antony ended that rivalry by confiscating its two hundred thousand scrolls and presenting them as a gift to Cleopatra. (The Ptolemies once cut off the export of papyrus to Pergamum, forcing its scholars to work on vellum made from sheepskin. Since vellum is more easily stacked than rolled, the result was volumes of bound sheets—the first "modern" books.)

The Alexandrian Library's fate is still a mystery. By most accounts it was heavily damaged or destroyed by fire. Roman writer Seneca is said to be the first to have commented on

it, expressing his pleasure over the burning of forty thousand "useless" scrolls.

At the end of the fourth century, Christian emperor Theodosius I ordered the Library's annex, the Temple of Serapis, to be burned because it was "pagan." Some two hundred thousand priceless scrolls went up in flames. Whatever scrolls survived their predations were burned for fuel by Arabs who swept through Egypt in A.D. 640.

The 4th-century assaults on the Library touched off the Dark Ages. The great knowledge gained in the fields of mathematics, astronomy, and applied sciences would not be begin to be recovered until the Renaissance and, sadly, many of its

magnificent literary treasures would remain forever lost to the world.

Left: Scholars study and workers return scrolls to their proper shelves in this 19th-century German print of a room in the Alexandria Library. The papyrus scrolls, rolled around dowels, were all carefully indexed and labeled.

Below: A detail from the Egyptian *Book of the Dead* suggests that there are still fields to plow in the afterlife. Despite its grim title, the *Book of the Dead,* which dates from the 13th century B.C., largely celebrates the richness of life and the survival of the soul.

When it came to learning, no son or daughter of the Ptolemaic line had ever been more passionate or dedicated than the young Princess Cleopatra VII, who was born in 69 B.C. It was the custom of her family to educate male and female children according to the same curriculum, since the throne was supposed to be shared by a brother and sister. The princess studied the classics of Greek literature, the rhetoric of Demosthenes, the histories of Thucydides and Herodotus. She showed particular aptitude for the sciences: arithmetic, geometry, astronomy, and medicine all interested her. She could draw well, sing, and play the seven-stringed lyre. She was also a physically gifted child, delighting in movement, a good dancer, and a superb horsewoman.

Easily mastering all the accomplishments expected of her, she sought more. She was the first of her long dynasty to learn Egyptian, and she was fluent in several other tongues of Africa and the Middle East, among them Ethiopian, Troglodyte, Hebrew, Aramaic, Syriac, Median, and Parthian.

Along with her considerable knowledge, young Cleopatra had wit, sublety, and a keen eye for the absurd. She was developing an intellect that was both incisive and patient, making her seem far older than her years. In the royal household, however, growing up could be dangerous. Given the Ptolemaic proclivity for winnowing out their own, some of the dynasty's children did not manage to get very old. Cleopatra knew this. Although she took immense pride in her family (the Ptolemies were, after all, among the oldest reigning dynasties on earth), she was well aware of how murderous they could be.

A marble and plaster head found in Alexandria is believed to depict Cleopatra's father, Ptolemy XII Auletes, whom she was said to greatly resemble. Scholars believe this piece was completed sometime after Auletes returned from exile and regained his throne in 55 B.C.

For this reason, among others, her childhood must have been an interplay of light and shadow. As a princess, she lived in fabled luxury; Egypt was owned by its rulers, and nothing in the nation was grown, manufactured, or traded without a share going to the royal household. She had her own sumptuous quarters, her own servants, her own horses, her own little boat for sailing the aquamarine waters of the private royal harbor. Her body was pampered with superb food and scented baths and the finest linens and imported silks, and her keen mind was nourished by the best tutors and greatest library in the world. But amid all this magnificence and privilege she was largely alone, isolated from the mass of people by her exalted station in life, and by certain family circumstances. Her mother had died before Cleopatra was even old enough to know her; and her brothers and sisters, being Ptolemies, were rivals, not friends.

She had two older sisters, Cleopatra VI and Berenice IV. (The Ptolemy women, like the men, shared a scant supply of names; all were called either Berenice, Arsinoë, or Cleopatra, which meant "glory to her father.") There were also three half-siblings by her father's second wife: Arsinoë IV, who was three years younger than Cleopatra VII, and two younger boys, Ptolemy XIII and Ptolemy XIV.

Arsinoë was considered the budding beauty of the family, but Cleopatra appears to have been her father's favorite. Doubtless he enjoyed her intelligence and humor—and treasured her loyalty: Of all the children, she was the one who seemed to truly love him. That cannot have always been easy, for Auletes was a complicated man.

"Auletes" was not a nickname of his choosing but one conferred on him by his people, and it expressed a certain contempt. He drank too much, and sometimes he was seen playing his flute in the streets in the company of common musicians—most unroyal behavior. His subjects also gave him another insulting name, Nothos, meaning "Bastard." It was accurate; he was the illegitimate son of Ptolemy IX by a concubine.

Like several of his predecessors, Auletes courted the favor of Rome, thus earning even more scorn from his own people. Yet he had no choice. Despite his weaknesses he was an intelligent and practical man, and a realist. Rome was now the master of the Mediterranean world. One by one, independent Hellenistic states had become Roman provinces. Egypt alone remained independent—but only on Roman sufferance and for Roman reasons: The new superpower had its own internal factions to contend with, and annexing Egypt would give any Roman who governed it a degree of wealth that could be dangerous.

For Auletes, the reality was obvious: He who would rule Egypt must deal with Rome. So he pursued a pro-Roman policy, one whose logic he would pass on to his favorite daughter. By the time Cleopatra was nearing adolescence, however, Auletes was finding it harder and harder to maintain his power. His public carousing and his subservience to Rome were causing a seething resentment in Egypt that bordered on outright rebellion. He had no choice but to turn to Rome for help.

The daughter must have watched the father's dilemma with a mixture of sympathy and fear, understanding why he drank so much and spent his nights in dissipation. He was living under terrible pressure.

Like many modern cities, ancient Alexandria was laid out in a grid. Cleopatra and her predecessors lived in the Royal Quarter, or Brucheion, now submerged, which fronted on the southeast coast of the Great Harbor. The illustration below (circa 1690) shows a harbor of the great city, by Johann Bernhard.

And so was she—she, who for all her precocious wisdom was still only a child. What if her beloved father were deposed or killed? What if power fell to one of her older sisters, Berenice or Cleopatra VI? To them, she could only have been a threat—too smart, too spirited, too likely to aspire to the throne herself.

And they were right about her aspirations. She was a Ptolemy too, after all, and ambition was a hallmark of the royal line. From childhood she had educated herself for the crown she might receive. Statecraft fascinated her, inspiring endless questions for her tutors. Would Rome let the Ptolemies keep Cyprus? Who would rule in Judea? Would the Roman civil wars ever end? Would there be a new dictator? Would it be the wealthy Crassus? Or Pompey the Great? Or that commanding general, Julius Caesar? She must also have learned from her father, seeing the guile and shrewdness behind his clownish exterior. It is not difficult to imagine her being summoned to his apartments, where he would confide to her his fears and hopes, his anxiety over Egypt's delicate balancing act in its relations with Rome. One can envision the young Cleopatra scampering barefoot across the polished onyx floor, past massive doors inlaid with tortoise shell and set with emeralds, to sit at his feet, listening attentively for hours. If he drank too much wine, she might oversee the servants as they prepared him for bed.

It can be supposed, too, that her father sometimes allowed her to stand by his throne as he received foreign ambassadors. She would be able to take in everything about them: their dress, their tone of voice, the deference or lack of it that denoted their degree of power. Perhaps Auletes sometimes even allowed her to say a few

CLEOPATRA'S MOTHER

Since ancient sources are silent on the matter, scholars have long puzzled over the question of who Cleopatra's mother was and what happened to her. Most likely, she was Cleopatra V, the wife and sister of Ptolemy XII Auletes, and she died either giving birth to Cleopatra VII or soon thereafter.

This conclusion is based on several facts that are known about the Ptolemies. First, they were, by ancient standards, conspicuously monogamous; very few of the kings had mistresses or concubines, and the queens were remarkably bereft of lovers. Doubtless this was less a matter of morality than of family honor: They took great pride in their royal lineage and were thus scrupulous about keeping the bloodline pure.

An even more persuasive argument for Cleopatra's being the daughter of a queen is the unaccustomed quiet of her critics. Once she became an enemy of Rome, Roman writers of the day hurled every possible insult at her, accusing her of all sorts of depravity, crime, and shortcomings. Had there been the slightest hint that her birth was illegitimate, they surely would have added bastardy to their arsenal of invectives.

Above: **A relief shows a woman seated in a *meskhenet*, or birthing chair. She is assisted by incarnations of the goddess Hathor, believed to bring a safe and easy delivery.**

words, welcoming a visitor in his native tongue. How she must have relished the look of surprise on the ambassador's face, the look of pride on her father's. Still, the precariousness of her childhood must have made her guarded, even with her father. She could have safely shared her dreams only with the dead.

Perhaps she did just that—and, if so, who would have made a more suitable confidant than the ancestor who, in spirit, she most resembled? It is tempting to picture such a moment: Dismissing her tutors and nurses, running down the marble steps of the palace, making her way along a broad thoroughfare to what was known simply as "The Tomb," ordering guards to shoo away the worshipers and tourists so that she could be alone with Alexander, the warrior whose legend somehow still presided over this city.

Standing on tiptoe, she could have studied his face. Her grandfather, the bloated Ptolemy IX, had melted down the con-

The artistic impulse in Egypt found expression in intricate jewelry.
Below-right: An inlaid ring of electrum, an alloy of gold and silver, dating from the 18th Dynasty, 1570–1293 B.C.
Below: An early Ptolemaic-period winged scarab pectoral whose wings contain the remains of glass paste inlay simulating lapis lazuli, felspar, and carnelian.

queror's golden sarcophagus to pay mercenaries, so enraging the Alexandrians that they had risen up and killed him. The gold had been replaced by a crystal dome that arched over the body, allowing an unobstructed view. The embalmers had done well; he was as beautiful in death as in life, his face and body now enhanced by a thin sheen of gold.

Perhaps, curling up beside the coffin, Cleopatra told Alexander of her fears and hopes. She would rule, and not just Egypt. She would restore all the lands the Ptolemies had held in the dynasty's prime. She would make Egypt glorious again, and feared as well. She would use the hated Romans to achieve these ends—and she would let them use her, if need be. But when all was said and done, Egypt would be Rome's partner, not its subject. Together, West and East, they would command the world.

"The strongest," the dying Alexander had said. She was strongest. Somehow, she would be queen.

Chapter II
PRINCESS & QUEEN

If she hoped to rule, Cleopatra had to reach adulthood, and for a time, her chances appeared slim. As would so often be the case, her fate was tangled in the web of Rome.

In 60 B.C., when the princess was nine years old, Rome's three most powerful men established an informal alliance called the First Triumvirate. All three belonged to the city's old aristocracy. One, Marcus Licinius Crassus, lacked the military credentials that were the usual ticket to power in Rome, but he had great wealth. The other two members of the alliance were both accomplished generals, Gnaeus Pompey and Gaius Julius Caesar.

Rome, which had done away with kings long before, prided itself on being a republic, ruled by the Senate and by pairs of consuls who served one-year terms.

Painter Alexandre Cabanel portrayed Cleopatra in a manner that became popular in the 19th century: as a woman in Egyptian costume. In actuality, Cleopatra probably only dressed in Egyptian garb during formal state occasions.

With the formation of the First Triumvirate, the republic was effectively finished. Several years would pass before the official burial, but the reality was that Crassus, Pompey, and Caesar now ruled Rome.

This reality had great significance for Auletes, whose kingship in Egypt was hanging by a thread. He was especially unpopular with his fellow Greeks in Alexandria, who—still unable to digest the fact that Rome controlled their destiny—considered their king a weakling. Facing a probable uprising, Auletes turned to Pompey and Caesar. The two triumvirs were happy to come to his aid—for a price, of course, and a high one: six thousand talents, the equivalent of Egypt's entire revenue for upwards of a year. The king agreed to their terms, and Caesar, who was consul at the time, obligingly passed a law declaring Egypt, under Auletes, a "friend and ally of the Roman people." This arrangement confirmed, for the time being, Egypt's nominal independence; it also implied that Roman legions would oppose any effort to dethrone the current king.

Pompey and Caesar wanted their huge payoff immediately, but Auletes needed time to prepare his restive subjects for the news of what he had done—namely, commited them to paying higher taxes for the privilege of keeping their detested monarch. His solution was to borrow the money from a Roman speculator named Gaius Rabirius, thereby piling interest on top of the already staggering debt. The whole affair was a desperate gamble, but a necessary one, as he saw it.

Cleopatra no doubt realized what her father was up to, and she must have watched with growing horror, knowing the outcry he would face when word got out of his arrangement with the hated Romans. Some small hope may have dawned as Auletes began trying in earnest to salvage his reputation, courting public favor with such popular moves as a declaration of general amnesty for all people facing prosecution.

Then came another crisis, greatly adding to the king's peril: Rome decided to annex Cyprus. The island kingdom belonged to Egypt, although it was ruled not by Auletes but by his brother, Ptolemy XI. The Romans made a casual offer to soften the blow by making the Cyprian Ptolemy high priest of Aphrodite at Paphos, but he sneered at the crumb. Rather than face being deposed by Rome, he killed himself.

All Egypt cheered Ptolemy's defiance and his courage, at the same time directing commensurate rage at Auletes for having done nothing to help his brother. This fury was reaching flood tide just when the public learned of the new taxes being levied to finance the royal bribe for Pompey and Caesar. At that point, the Egyptians made it clear that they'd had enough. They would endure no more of Auletes. The people revolted, and the king had to flee Alexandria.

With her father no longer there to protect her, Cleopatra faced a future more fraught with dangers than ever. Egypt was in chaos, with the turbulence extending to the very pinnacle of power. Most Egyptians considered Auletes' rightful successor to be his eldest daughter, Cleopatra VI Tryphaena ("She Who Lives in Luxury"). In other circles, however, Berenice IV, the second sister, was regarded as queen. Each sister had her circle of courtiers, and each vied for support to bolster her claim to the throne.

Then, suddenly, Cleopatra Tryphaena was gone—vanished. No one could be sure exactly what had happened to her, but it was rumored that she had been killed on the orders of Berenice. Those rumors would have quickly reached the ears of Auletes' third daughter, Cleopatra VII, and she must have wondered whether she would be next—strangled in the night by one of Berenice's henchmen, perhaps, or the victim of some mysterious ailment brought on by poison in her food. As days and weeks of dread crawled by, the princess most likely tried to make herself inconspicuous—playing with her horses, burying herself in her schoolwork, perhaps even binding her developing body to make it look as childish as possible. Her best hope for survival was to seem too frivolous, too bookish, too young—altogether too unimportant to require killing.

It was impossible for her to be entirely invisible, of course; there were occasions when she couldn't avoid seeing her sister the queen. At these times Cleopatra must have been deferential and submissive, swearing her undying affection and loyalty. It was the princess' good fortune that Berenice was turning out to be the most unsubtle of Ptolemies. Apparently concluding that Cleopatra was beneath her notice for the moment, she focused all her attention on acquiring a husband. Possibly she was trying to solidify her rule; or perhaps the queen just wanted a man.

Ptolemaic queens had ruled alone from time to time, but the practice ran against tradition; they were supposed to share the throne with a king. Tradition also directed the marriage of siblings, but here Berenice rebelled, declining even nominal wedlock with either of her two preadolescent brothers. Instead, she looked outside Egypt for a mate. Successive betrothals to two Seleucid princes fell through, and

ROMAN GOVERNMENT

When Rome dispensed with kings toward the end of the sixth century B.C., the city-state became a republic, governed primarily by the Senate. Its membership varied in number, but there were usually several hundred senators. Traditionally, these men were patriarchs of Rome's patrician clans.

The oligarchical power of the aristocracy was coveted by the other class of Roman citizens, the plebeians, who included farmers, laborers, and tradesmen. The plebeians had their own legislative body, the Assembly. Originally, the Assembly had little authority, and the laws it passed applied only to plebeians. Over the years, however, the plebeians chipped away at aristocratic dominance. By Julius Caesar's time, laws made by the Assembly applied to all Romans, and one of the two consuls who served one-year terms and enjoyed supreme authority had to be a plebeian. Since consuls joined the Senate after their terms ended, it was possible for a plebeian to be a senator.

Above: **Detail from an 1889 fresco by Cesare Maccari:** *Cicero, in the Senate, Accusing Cataline of Conspiracy.*

The Ptolemies often had themselves depicted in traditional Egyptian style with the ruler wearing the ritual beard, *above.* Even female pharaohs were represented in this manner. *Right:* A figure of a Ptolemaic queen. Women of the royal family held the honor of legitimizing the "son of god," or the earthly Horus. They held important and influential positions, even assuming the regency for their minor sons in the event of the pharaoh's death.

a brief union with a third proved highly unsatisfactory: He was so boorish that the Alexandrians called him Cybiosactes ("Salt-fishmonger"). Berenice, evidently sharing the popular view, endured him for only three days before having him strangled.

In the second year of her reign, the queen settled on a man named Archelaus, the illegitimate son of a former king of Pontus in Asia Minor. Archelaus was reasonably attractive, and he seemed strong enough to help his new wife repel any foreign invasion that might occur. This last consideration was telling, for Berenice had married him without even seeking, much less receiving, approval from Rome. That, she would find, was a mistake.

Although Egypt was still unsettled, some semblance of normality was returning. Berenice had avoided making enemies within the kingdom, and with a king by her side, she appeared to have a secure hold on the throne. The greatest threat to her reign would come from outside Egypt—from her own father, living in exile. She and her supporters had discounted him: He was gone, he would stay gone, and that was that. In assuming so, however, they wagered too heavily on his weakness and paid too little heed to some other traits he had demonstrated over the years—cunning, tenacity, and ruthlessness. Those sides of his character now came into play. He was plotting his return.

When Auletes fled Egypt, he had headed for Rome, there to collect on his costly arrangement with Pompey and Caesar. Caesar was off fighting in Gaul, but Pompey received the deposed king graciously, although he seemed in no particular hurry to raise an army to restore Auletes to his throne. The speculator Rabirius was in a hurry, however, since he was the man who had lent the Egyptian king the original bribe money to pay off the triumvirs. Auletes owed him a fortune, and Rabirius nagged Pompey constantly, reminding him that a ruling king was far more likely to pay his debt than an exiled one. Pompey saw his point. Besides, the triumvir was more than a little irritated that Queen Berenice had installed as king of Egypt a husband that he himself had no part in choosing.

As a preemptive move, Auletes' enemies in Alexandria dispatched a contingent of one hundred men to Italy to try to talk the Romans out of helping the deposed monarch. Auletes, probably with Pompey's help, had most of them murdered as soon as they disembarked; the survivors found themselves reluctant to say anything hostile. That done, Auletes headed for the world's most sacred place of sanctuary, the temple of Artemis at Ephesus, leaving the Romans to sort out who was going to help him and how. It seemed certain that one of them would; the Romans had a long history of acting in their own best interests.

And they did on this occasion. In due course, Pompey turned over the job of Auletes' restoration to one Aulus Gabinius, governor of the Roman province of Syria, recently grabbed from the Seleucids. Again, there was a prodigious price for the services the Romans were supposed to provide: Auletes would have to pay Gabinius (with cuts to Caesar and Pompey) ten thousand talents, a sum that would beggar even Egypt's treasury. The king probably had no idea how he would raise the money, nor would he particularly have cared, shrewdly reasoning that the higher the sum, the harder the Romans would work to collect it.

Setting out from Judea, Gabinius attacked Egypt from the east. His chief cavalry officer, a young Roman named Mark Antony, easily captured the frontier fort of Pelusium. From there, Gabinius marched toward Alexandria. Berenice's new husband, Archelaus, led the forces of opposition, but to little avail. He died in battle. Gabinius easily won the day, and Auletes regained his throne.

The king's return was hardly cause for jubilation for most Alexandrians, but Cleopatra was surely overjoyed. She had her cherished father back, and the months of hiding from her sister and cringing in her presence were over.

Consistent with his nature, Auletes would probably have hosted a banquet to celebrate his restoration, and his fourteen-year-old daughter would have been the happiest of celebrants. If such an occasion occurred, history conceals the details, but the scene can be imagined:

The feast would have been held in the king's enormous banquet hall. There, hundreds of guests, including Gabinius and his officers, would have lounged on couches in the Roman fashion, drinking fine Falernian wine from golden cups and dining from gold plates encrusted with jewels. The fare would have been planned to satisfy even the fabled appetites of the Romans: roast ox and wild boar, succulent oysters steamed in seaweed, baked fish and shellfish, and even crocodile and hippopotamus; the meat of peacocks and flamingos, quail and thrush; and for dessert pastries drenched in honey, rich custard, grapes, dates, and figs, and berries cooled with snow imported from Thrace. The Romans may have disapproved of such ostentation, but they could hardly have been unimpressed.

Cleopatra would have dressed for the occasion with great care. One can picture her in a gown in the Grecian style, a rich silk, the threads of the fabric laboriously pulled and separated by hand to enhance its sheer, diaphanous quality. Perhaps she chose Egyptian jewelry: wide, gold bands on her upper arms; an intricate collar of gold, lapis, malachite, turquoise, and carnelian; and on her forehead the slender, gold diadem of an Egyptian princess. She would have wanted to look her best so her father could present her with pride to the Roman visitors.

Behind history's veil, the celebration of the king's return may have gone well, delighting all the guests and redounding to the glory of its host. But perhaps not: This, after all, was a ruler whose judgment could be dangerously faulty. A dark turn to the evening is therefore worth envisioning, too.

A pectoral from the 4th century B.C. and a cuff bracelet from around 1000 B.C. show the intricacy of Egyptian jewelry. Like most fine jewelry of the time, they are made of gold, a metal more readily available than silver in ancient Egypt.

Even the stiff Romans, responding to the magnificent food and drink and exultant over their military victory, probably laughed, exchanged toasts, bantered with one another. But given Auletes' fondness for wine, his need to behave with dignity in front of these outlanders may not have been met. Perhaps Auletes called for his flute, lifted it to his lips and began to play. Perhaps, enraptured by his own melody, he rose from his couch, moved to the middle of the now-hushed chamber, and began to dance.

The Romans would have been dumbstruck. To them, dancing was disgraceful, a sign of drunkenness and degeneracy. But Auletes was known to behave this way in public, and so he might have on this night—the king of Egypt, dancing before the Romans, swaying and twirling like some common sot in the streets. It would have been yet another instance of culture shock between West and East: The foreigners could never have understood that what seemed to them debauchery was, for Auletes, worship.

MAKING FACES

Cosmetics were already an ancient tradition in both Greece and Egypt in Cleopatra's time. Ground minerals, such as the greenish-black galena, were used to darken and define the eyelids; ochre could tint the lips. Egyptian women would stain their nails, the soles of their feet, and their palms a reddish hue with henna, which was also used as a hair dye.

Hellenistic women rubbed white lead powder into their skin to make it fairer, and they used extracts of various plants and seaweeds to create rouges for their lips and cheeks.

Cleopatra must have known all about such methods, and her own makeup was probably elaborate. An ancient treatise on cosmetic arts was attributed to her. It's doubtful that she wrote it personally, but the use of her name was probably meant as a tribute to her beauty and her artistry with paints and powders.

Above: Detail from a stela of the glamorous princess Nefertiabet, 2500 B.C.

Above right: An alabaster cosmetic spoon shaped like a leaf. The arching duck's head that makes up the handle was a common decorative device on cosmetic tools.

Found among the shipwreck artifacts were two rings, *above*, most likely from a post-Ptolemaic period. One, entirely of gold, is topped by a decorative pyramid. Set into the other gold ring is a blue chalcedony stone, a type of quartz. The stone features an intaglio, or engraving, the impression of which would yield an image in relief.

Right: Cleopatra's jewelry collection—which was no doubt massive—probably included, along with Egyptian styles, more delicate Greek pieces similar to those shown at right. Animal heads were a common motif, as was the knot of Hercules, used in the piece in the center, once part of a diadem, or royal headband.

Ptolemy XII had never called himself "Auletes." The name he had taken was Philopater Neos Dionysus—"He Who Loves His Father, the New Dionysus." He considered Dionysus his patron, and himself the god's avatar on earth. The Romans equated Dionysus with their Bacchus, god of wine and revelry, but in the East he was something quite different: a god of transcendence, of mystical ecstasy, of resurrection and immortality, associated in the Egyptian mind with Osiris. He was a beloved god, and his followers worshiped him with music and dancing.

But the Romans were never much for nuance. And if indeed Auletes, warmed with wine, honored his god this night with his flute and his body, they would have seen only a drunk making a public spectacle of himself. Shock and disgust would have registered on each Roman face—all, perhaps, but one. Mark Antony, the handsome, black-haired young cavalry officer, was known to be fond of exotic Greek ways. One can picture him reclining on his couch on an elbow, a half-smile on his lips, his head moving gently in time with the music, actually enjoying it.

If so, the keenly observant Cleopatra would have noticed, and been grateful to him—grateful for his help in delivering her father at Pelusium and for his refusal to judge him now.

An Attic red-figure painting on the inside of a circa-510 B.C. kylix— a shallow, footed bowl with handles, used for drinking wine—shows a flute player and a dancer. In ancient times, some people believed that flute players had magical powers.

The rest of Alexandria definitely had reason to be grateful to Antony, Roman though he was. When Berenice's husband, Archelaus, died in battle, Auletes had been all for letting him rot on the battlefield—the worst insult that one Greek could inflict on another. It was Antony who insisted on a decent burial. It was also Antony who prevented Auletes' wholesale slaughter of captured Egyptian prisoners. Alexandrians concluded from these acts that the tall, heavily muscled young captain had a good heart and a generous nature. But even Antony couldn't save Berenice. Auletes would not forgive his daughter's treason, and he ordered her killed.

There is no way of knowing how Cleopatra felt about the execution, whether she experienced grief or satisfaction. Satisfaction seems more likely: She might have expected no better at the hands of her sister. Besides, Berenice had been a traitor to her father and a usurper. To a Ptolemy, it must have seemed right that she should die.

It was also convenient. This latest Ptolemaic power struggle had left Cleopatra as Auletes' eldest surviving child, first in line for the throne.

The civil strife had other consequences as well. Gabinius and Rabirius set about wringing as much money out of Egypt as they could. Rabirius even got himself appointed to a high government post, the better to carry out his looting. He soon aroused such

In painting his 1877 version of an Egyptian feast in Cleopatra's day, English Orientalist Edwin Long suffered from several misconceptions. Most notably, he has the diners sitting on chairs, in proper British fashion. In fact, Cleopatra's banquets would have been in the Graeco-Roman style, with feasters reclining on couches situated alongside the banquet tables. Each couch accommodated three people, and the diners usually propped themselves on the left elbow and ate with the right hand. Long, working from an ancient account by the Greek biographer Plutarch, also shows servants dragging a mummy on a sled around the banquet room. Here the mistake was Plutarch's; he believed that all Egyptian banquets ended with this ritual. In fact, the mummy made his grim appearance only at funeral feasts, where the intention was to remind the guests of their own mortality.

GOD OF ECSTASY

Born of Zeus by a mortal woman, Dionysus was the god who gave humans the gift of growing grapes and making wine. To the Greeks, however, he was not a god of drunkenness but of ecstatic transcendence, of mystical revelation achieved by the shedding of inhibitions. (The Greek roots of the word *ecstasy* literally mean "to stand outside oneself.") Wine was one path to ecstasy, but not the only one: As this fifth-century Attic red-figure vase painting of Dionysus playing a lyre suggests, music and dance were others, and both were part of his worship.

The cult of Dionysus was a mystery religion; that is, its followers were initiated into mysteries that were not to be shared with unbelievers. Some of these secrets probably had to do with fertility, since Dionysus was a god of the earth and of vegetation.

Some Greeks were dismayed by his popularity, considering his influence a threat to good order: His followers, most of them women, seemed to lose all reason when celebrating his rites. For believers, however, Dionysus was the bringer of joy in this life and the promise of immortality to come. It was probably for this reason that Egyptians came to equate him with Osiris, Lord of the Afterlife.

loathing in Alexandria that he had to flee for his life. He and Gabinius returned to Rome, where they were prosecuted for financial chicanery that overstepped even the liberal parameters set by the triumvirs. Gabinius was condemned and exiled. Rabirius somehow managed an acquittal, then wailed that he'd been reduced to poverty by Auletes' failure to pay his debt. So, turning his attention momentarily from his exploits to the north, Julius Caesar offered graciously (and for a fee) to take up the collection matter himself, once he had finished conquering Gaul—a promise that would eventually prove momentous for Cleopatra.

Another consequence of Auletes' restoration was the presence in Egypt of a sizable army of mercenaries. These were Gabinius' men—mostly tall, fair Germans and hardy Gauls—who had stayed behind when their leader left. Called the Gabinians, they were now in the service of the Egyptian crown. Auletes, dispelling whatever notion remained in the popular mind that he was merely a buffoon, kept the Gabinians under tight rein. He was able to use them as a threat to stifle the remaining discontent in the country, much of it emanating from Alexandrian merchants and delta farmers, who had suffered the depredations of Rabirius.

Perhaps chastened by his ouster and exile, Auletes seemed intent on putting his house in

Falcon-headed Egyptian god Horus is garbed as a Roman soldier in this 1st-century A.D. Roman statuette, *below.* From ancient times, Horus was associated with the military might of the pharaohs. Here the god wears the *nemes,* the headdress usually seen on sphinxes. Among mortals, the *nemes* could only be worn by pharaohs. *Following spread:* Roland Savoye films Fernand Pereira holding an artifact to be taken to the surface.

order, as both a king and a father. He resumed an impressive program of public works, erecting new buildings and restoring temples. It was as if he meant to show that he was a Ptolemy for good as well as ill—that while he could be as murderous and decadent as some of his ancestors, he could also leave behind, as they had, things of enduring value.

Although he was barely into his fifties, his days as an earthly king were drawing to a close. As his health began to fail, he took steps to ensure the orderly continuation of the dynasty. He composed a will, decreeing that the crown of Egypt would pass to his eldest daughter, and that she would ascend the throne in the company of her ten-year-old brother, Ptolemy XIII.

One copy of the will was kept under seal in Alexandria. In accordance with recent Ptolemaic practice, another was sent to Rome for safekeeping. It was placed into the hands of Pompey. In his testament, Auletes exhorted the Romans to honor their alliance with Egypt by making sure that his wishes were carried out.

Shortly after completing this duty, Ptolemy XII Auletes passed on to whatever fate Dionysus had in store. As he had decreed, his eldest daughter and her brother jointly inherited the kingdom. At the age of eighteen, Cleopatra VII Philopater, "She Who Loves Her Father," was queen of Egypt.

For the moment.

Chapter III
WOMAN & LOVER

Like all of her Ptolemaic predecessors, Cleopatra was elevated to the throne in a Greek-style coronation at Alexandria, but other, far older rites were held at Memphis, the ancient capital just upriver from the delta. In those ceremonies, she was invested with the crook and flail that Egyptian pharaohs had carried for millennia, and on her head was placed the double pharaonic crown: the white, bulbous crown of Upper Egypt, called the Lady of Dread, and the small red crown of Lower Egypt, known as the Lady of Spells.

There was also a crown with a vulture's head, and a gold circlet bearing the head of a cobra. The little cobra diadem, with its delicately wrought asp's head, was especially beautiful and rich in lore. The cobra had been a symbol of Egypt since time immemorial, and its lethal

A bas-relief, believed to be Ptolemaic, shows a queen as Isis-Hathor greeting a pharaoh. Cleopatra often had herself depicted as Isis, with the Hathor headdress, as did Ptolemaic queens before her.

bite was said to transport an Egyptian ruler instantly and painlessly to immortal life in the care of the gods.

More than any of her ancestors, Cleopatra expressed an affinity with pharaonic Egypt, a land old beyond reckoning, ancient before Greece was even born. She seemed to take almost as much pride in its traditions as she did in her own Greek heritage. Otherwise, it seems unlikely that she alone among the Ptolemies would have bothered to learn Egyptian, or that she would have taken such pains to better understand her eight million or so native subjects, most of whom lived outside Alexandria. She appeared to know, as Alexander knew long before, that kingship was precarious when a cultural gulf separated the ruling class from the native populace. That chasm certainly existed at the time of her coronation: In more than

SYMBOLS OF POWER

The reigning pharaoh of Egypt was the omnipresent Lord of Two Lands (Lower and Upper Egypt). Regarded not only as the supreme ruler but as a god, he was worshiped as Horus, the son of the god Osiris. The pharaoh's kingship was not merely a duty or privilege derived from a superhuman force, it was absolute, divine. And to that divine station was given the charge of administering the principles of the goddess Maat—truth, justice, and balance—as well as ensuring the sense of continuity and prosperity to the kingdom. Bestowed upon all living pharaohs were the royal insignias: the crook and flail, symbols of benevolence and royal dominance; the double crown—the red crown of Lower Egypt (northern) and the white crown of Upper Egypt (southern) put together to represent a unified Egypt— and the nemes, the traditional striped headcloth. These symbols of royalty, among others, often adorned members of the royal family as well, as depicted in this 19th-Dynasty relief from Karnak showing the divination of Ahmes Nerfertari, wife of Ramses the Great, holding the flail, *near right*. Atop her head she wears a small crown, called the *modius,* made up of a ring of cobra heads. Above it are the horns of the goddess Hathor, enclosing a solar disk. On her forehead Nefertari wears both the royal cobra, symbolic of the king and kingdom of Lower Egypt, and a vulture's head, emblematic of the mother goddess Mut. Completing the headdress are Mut's vulture wings, extending back behind the queen's ears.

Opposite: **A detail from a tomb painting shows Osiris as Lord of the West. (The Netherworld, home of the dead, was believed to lie within the region of the setting sun.) Osiris carries both the royal flail and the crook. On his head is the bulbous white crown of Upper Egypt, adorned by two ostrich feathers. The four small figures standing on the lotus in front of the god are the sons of Horus; they protected the internal organs of the mummy after mummification.**

two and a half centuries of Ptolemaic rule, Egypt's two cultures—one indigenous, one Greek—remained widely disparate, and often at odds with each other.

Some amalgamation had occurred, of course. It was obvious in Egypt's art and architecture, and over the years there had been a certain amount of intermarriage, even though unions between Greeks and native Egyptians weren't recognized legally. Still, Hellenism was really no more than a thin veneer atop Egypt's ancient customs and beliefs. Religion, in particular, had proved deeply resistant to change. The complex and colorful tapestry of Egyptian gods—major gods and minor, local gods and national gods, gods grafted onto one another, gods revered in combination as well as separately, gods in human form and gods with the heads of falcons or jackals or cows or crocodiles, gods who governed every tiny facet of life—was all but impenetrable to foreigners. No matter what conquerors came and went, the gods kept Egypt's heart safe and sacrosanct, immune to all intruders.

Paradoxically, though, the very religion that separated Egypt's native masses from their Greek overlords was also the factor that most explained why Egyptians tolerated the Ptolemies: The religion needed monarchs. The pharaohs had been the links between earth and heaven—gods themselves and the intermediaries between gods and mortals. In the absence of the native pharaohs, the new kings and queens, Greek though they were, would have to do. So while the Egyptians generally disliked their foreign rulers, who kept them an economically depressed underclass, they also worshiped them. And the priests, the leaders of the native population, cooperated with the Ptolemy regimes.

The first Ptolemy had realized the importance of religion and, attempting to lay a popular foundation for his dynasty, had tried to woo Egypt by honoring the country's deities—merging some of them with Greek divinities, and decreeing that his successors should respect the Egyptian gods and maintain their temples. To one degree or another, all of them had done so, and the arrangement had worked well enough. Despite occasional uprisings and even a few efforts in Middle Egypt or Upper Egypt to install competing native dynasties, the Greeks had been able to maintain control of their far more numerous native subjects.

Auletes had been particularly diligent about the temples. Among his many works was the restoration of the temple of Amon-Re, king of the gods, at Karnak in Upper Egypt's ancient city of Thebes. Founded as a small shrine almost two thousand years earlier, Karnak had become for a time the largest and most splendid place of worship the world had ever known, and bringing it back to its former glory won him considerable affection among the Egyptians.

Queen Cleopatra, following her father's policy in religion as in many other things, set out shortly after her coronation to associate herself as closely as possible with the native gods. And fate provided her with an excellent opportunity.

The most famous deity in Upper Egypt at the time was the sacred bull Buchis, worshiped as the soul of Amon-Re and kept within the sacred precincts of Hermonthis, a few miles south of Thebes. Every time the holy bull died, it was replaced with a new one amid much solemn ceremony. Although the Ptolemies had traditionally sent emissaries to these rites, no ruler had ever gone in person. But when Buchis died in 51 B.C., Cleopatra traveled up the Nile to install his replacement. It was a popular move, and she was hailed by the locals not merely as Cleopatra VII Philopater, but as the Lady of the Two Lands, Cleopatra Thea Philopater—"the Goddess Who Loves Her Father."

For the young queen, the visit to Hermonthis was almost certainly more than a political gesture. Like her father and so many other Ptolemies, she was something of a paradoxical creature—a hard-headed pragmatist and at the same time a devout mystic. Leading the magnificent young bull among the ranks of the assembled priests, she must have felt the pride and the burden of knowing that for them she was Isis incarnate, a goddess on earth.

GODS OF EGYPT

So vital was Egypt's religion to its people that its pantheon of gods was always growing and changing. Over the nation's long history, the relative importance of various deities would shift from time to time and from place to place. Thus a major god of the 4th Dynasty might enjoy only secondary status by the 19th Dynasty, or a god all-important in Thebes would be only a minor deity in Lower Egypt.

To further complicate this shifting tapestry, the attributes and duties of one divinity might closely resemble those of another, so that eventually the two would come to be worshiped together, or even to merge into a single entity. And foreign influences would bring new gods to join with the old.

The very elasticity of the Egyptian faith gave it great durability, for it lasted more than three thousand years. And the worship of one of its major figures, the goddess Isis, persisted well into the Christian era, long after other pagan deities were abandoned and forgotten.

In addition to the more prominent Egyptian deities—Osiris, God of the Afterlife, and his sister and wife Isis, the giver of life and mother of Horus—a variety of other Egyptian gods who were important during Cleopatra's time are depicted on the following pages.

Below: A mummiform figure of three gods in one—

Ptah, Sokar, and Osiris—faces the falcon god Horus in this funerary statue from an Egyptian tomb, circa 200 B.C. Ptah was a creator god, Sokar a god of cemeteries, and Osiris the God of the Dead. Ptah-Sokar-Osiris statues were often hollow, so that magical spells written on papyrus could be placed inside to help protect the dead. The role of Horus, the falcon-headed sky god who was the offspring of Isis and Osiris, was also protective. Carved into the base of the statue are ankhs, symbols of life, alternating with *was* scepters, staffs of power. These assured the dead of life and power in the next world.

Right: This limestone bas-relief appears on a stela that once served to consecrate a royal foundation. On the far right, a pharaoh, wearing the royal kilt and the double crown of Egypt, holds out *nu* pots filled with beer or wine to placate Sekhmet, the lion-headed goddess of destruction, and her son Heka, whose name means "magical power." A queen, wearing a crown and headdress that suggest the goddess Hathor, stands opposite Sekhmet and plays the *sistrum,* a musical instrument sacred to Hathor. Given its position in front of the pharaoh it is possible this figure represents Cleopatra VII. At the top, two cobras hang from a winged solar disk, protecting the rulers below.

This depiction of an Apis bull, *above left,* was probably made in Alexandria's famous glassworks under the Ptolemies. The Apis was likely the only animal in Egyptian religion that was a god itself, not merely the symbol of a god. The divine bull was supposedly conceived when lightning struck a cow, and it could be recognized by special markings: the shape of the wings on the back and the sacred scarab beetle on the tongue. There was only one Apis bull at any one time, and during its life it enjoyed a pampered existence inside a temple. When it died, it was mummified and placed in a special burial chamber at Saqqara called the *Serapeum.*
Above: The head depicts Hathor with the ears of a cow, her sacred animal. A goddess of love, Hathor was also associated with music, particularly with a sistrum, a kind of rattle that was often made in the shape of her head. She was one of the few Egyptian deities that were customarily portrayed full-face rather than in profile. Another was Bes, a dwarf-like god of war and childbirth. In Egypt's later history, Hathor became closely associated with Isis.

Left: A composition statuette glazed in turquoise and dark blue shows Isis suckling the infant Horus. Her crown is a throne, from which her name is derived: The Egyptian word for throne was *ist*, which the Greeks changed to Istis and later Isis.

Top right: This green marble figurine depicts the falcon-headed god Horus with the body of a crocodile, one of his many various forms. To Egyptians of the time, the baboons adorning the base identified Horus as being a god of the sun itself.

Right: Sekhmet, daughter of the powerful sun god Re and wife of Ptah, was the lioness-headed goddess of war and destruction. Created by the fire of the eye of Re, Sekhmet was a weapon of vengeance used to destroy humankind for its wicked ways and disobedience to Re.

The queen probably savored the pilgrimage to Upper Egypt for yet another reason: It was a chance to get away from Alexandria, where she enjoyed neither love nor worship. She was, in fact, largely despised by her own people, the Alexandrian Greeks. The contempt that the Graeco-Egyptians had felt for her father and his pro-Roman policies had devolved upon her, and she had other troubles besides. One of the major ones had to do, once again, with Rome.

Two years before Cleopatra's accession, Crassus, the associate of Pompey and Caesar in the First Triumvirate, had set about trying to prove that he had the military talent to justify his exalted status in Rome. Instead, he managed to show what an inept general he really was. In a campaign against the Parthians, whose empire bordered the Roman province of Syria, Crassus was killed and his army routed. The Parthians then invaded Syria and occupied part of the country. Eventually, the Roman governor there, Marcus Calpurnius Bibulus, turned to Cleopatra for help.

Bibulus sent his two sons to appeal to the new queen of Egypt for the use of the Gabinian mercenaries, whose services she had inherited from Auletes. Cleopatra was willing, but the Gabinians themselves were not. They were thoroughly comfortable in Egypt, had no interest in leaving, and decided that killing Bibulus' sons was the most direct way to make their sentiments clear. Outraged, the queen had the murderers arrested and sent to Bibulus for punishment, thereby earning the enmity of her own army—and greatly increasing the risk that the soldiers would join with her dissatisfied Greek subjects to overthrow her.

Even nature seemed to conspire against her. The Nile, whose life-giving annual flood was so essential to the economy, stubbornly refused to rise. Crops were poor and famine threatened.

Perhaps if she'd been older and more experienced, Cleopatra

Because of the sculpting limitations of stone, the long, slender neck and curved beak that once topped this ibis body of the god Thoth were most likely fashioned out of wood or bronze. *Below:* An illustration of an ibis. *Following spread:* This view of Luxor Temple was painted by the German Carl Werner in 1870. Prominent is the colonnade of the 18th-Dynasty pharaoh Amenhotep III. The largest boat is a *dahebiah*, a craft commonly used by tourists visiting Egypt in the 19th century.

would have coped better with the various troubles besetting her. As it was, however, she let her pride and ambition overcome her good sense. At a time when her people were in no mood for such a thing, she made it all too clear that she meant to rule Egypt alone.

Although tradition decreed that Ptolemaic kings and queens reigned jointly, the queen always took second place to her consort. If the king was much younger, as was the case with Cleopatra's brother Ptolemy XIII, a regency council represented him, sharing power with the queen until the boy came of age. Flouting both custom and her father's will, Cleopatra ignored the existence of her brother and his council. She excluded Ptolemy from public ceremonies, made decisions of state on her own, and even minted coins that bore her portrait only, with no reference to him.

It might have seemed to her that Egypt, her dynasty, and her own destiny demanded no less, for the spoiled and self-indulgent Ptolemy was clearly her inferior in intelligence and discipline; it seemed unlikely that he would ever acquire the virtues of a good monarch. As for the regency council, its leader was a person the queen loathed and distrusted: Ptolemy's tutor, the eunuch Pothinus. This tall, gawky ibis of a man, with his oiled ringlets, bejeweled robes, and exaggerated makeup that would have embarrassed an Egyptian whore, was a constant threat to her throne. He may have looked absurd, but he was shrewd and single-minded, and he had considerable support.

Pothinus was able to rally all the disaffected elements in Egypt—the army, the natives who were suffering because of the failure of their crops, and, most notably, the Alexandrian Greeks, who had hated the queen all along. To them he needed only point out that the young king was weak and easily manipulated, traits that could never be attributed to his willful and headstrong sister, who was likely to hand Egypt over to Rome at her first opportunity.

The queen lost ground steadily. After the affair of Bibulus' sons, she was forced to at least make a public show of including Ptolemy as her royal colleague. The alternative, she must have known, was to face a popular uprising of the sort that had dethroned her father.

Once again she was alone and surrounded by enemies, as she had been when she was a child. Every day brought new variants of intrigue and danger, and her power, never firmly established, seemed to evanesce into mist, a mocking ghost that eluded every attempt to grasp it.

As the power of the regency council steadily eclipsed hers, assassination became a palpable threat. Fearing for her life, Cleopatra fled Alexandria, accompanied only by a few of her most trusted servants. She had held her throne for scarcely three years.

※

While the struggle in Egypt unfolded, a far more portentous battle for political control was underway in Rome. The whole Mediterranean world would feel its reverberations, and the life of the beleaguered queen would be profoundly affected.

Romans had already learned that the republic couldn't function for long with two powerful men at its head. Only a generation before, the ambitious leaders Sulla and Marius had pitched the nation into civil war as they fought for supremacy. Now the drama was being repeated. This time the combatants were Julius Caesar and Pompey the Great. Most knowledgeable observers predicted that Pompey would emerge the winner.

Coins struck in the image of Cleopatra VII, *right*, and her brother Ptolemy XIII.

Born into a distinguished patrician family, Pompey had known his first taste of civil strife during the war between Sulla and Marius, when he was only seventeen. He had fought for the victorious Sulla, eventually destroying all remnants of the Marian party in Africa, Sicily, and Spain. It was his exploits in Africa and Sicily that won him the sobriquet *Magnus,* "the Great."

In 71 B.C. he returned to Italy to quell the rebellion led by the Thracian slave Spartacus. The following year he served as consul, along with Crassus. After his three-year term in office ended, Pompey took his fame to new heights by clearing the Mediterranean of pirates and adding Pontus, Armenia, and Syria to Rome's eastern possessions. In light of these deeds, he was furious when the Senate refused his request to grant certain lands to his soldiers, and he abandoned the patrician party to align himself with Caesar and Crassus in the First Triumvirate. To help seal the pact, the aging hero had married Caesar's only daughter, Julia.

Julia's death in 54 B.C., and Crassus' the following year in his abortive campaign against the Parthians, spelled an end to stability. Corrosive jealousies arose between Pompey and Caesar, and a showdown appeared to be inevitable.

In Rome itself, Pompey was easily the more popular of the two contenders with both the Senate and the people. He had stayed in the city, taking care of his own political interests, during the nine years Caesar was off fighting in Gaul. But the younger general's phenomenal success in battle, and the huge fortune he was amassing from his conquests, made him a dangerous rival.

Pompey and most of the Senate feared Caesar's ambition and his growing power, so they ordered him to disband his army and return to Rome. Knowing that obeying could well mean his death, Caesar took a momentous gamble: Instead of disbanding his legions, he marched them across the Rubicon, the little river separating Gaul and Italy. For a general to enter Italy at the head of an army was a declaration of war; thus Rome once again found itself torn in two.

Rebounding from defeats in a few initial skirmishes, Caesar's forces drove Pompey and his supporters out of Italy. They fled to

Ptolemy XIII

Cleopatra VII

CLEOPATRA'S NEEDLES

It is a common misconception that Cleopatra had any connection to the two granite obelisks that once marked the entrance to the Caesarium. The name Cleopatra's Needles was a popular folkloric reference given to the nearly seventy-foot-tall monuments, perhaps originating from the belief that Cleopatra undertook the building of the Caesarium in honor of either Julius Caesar or Mark Antony, also a misconception. Dedication text found on them records the obelisks as having been erected in the eighteenth year of Octavian's reign, long after the queen's death.

The twin pillars survived the destruction of the Caesareum in A.D. 912. In the ensuing centuries they remained local landmarks, even after one was toppled by an earthquake and left to lie where it fell. In the nineteenth century, Egypt gave one of the obelisks to England and the other to America. Unfortunately, shipping and handling were not included, and the stories of the two monuments' journeys are sagas in themselves.

The one bound for England left Alexandria on September 21, 1877, towed behind the British ship *Olga* in a specially made wooden casing. During a terrible storm off the coast of Portugal, the obelisk had to be cut loose, but its watertight casing kept it afloat. It was found by a Scottish ship, which claimed right of salvage and charged the British government £2,000 to buy it back. In all, the government paid another £15,000 to import the monument and erect it on the banks of the Thames.

Industrialist William Vanderbilt financed the moving of the obelisk bound for America, promising an adventurer named Henry Honeychurch Gorringe $75,000 if he could get it safely from Alexandria to New York. Gorringe bought an Egyptian postal steamer and set out on the journey. On September 16, 1880, the obelisk entered the Hudson River and landed at 96th Street in Manhattan. Railroad tracks had to be laid from there to Central Park, the obelisk's eventual home. It was winched along the tracks by a steam engine, moving at the glacial rate of one city block a day. It took five months for Cleopatra's Needle to reach its final resting place.

Left: An 1838 lithograph depicting the obelisks, one standing, one fallen, after a painting by Scottish artist David Roberts.

A painting attributed to 19th-century French artist Theodore Gericault depicts the murder of Pompey the Great by henchmen of Ptolemy XIII. Stabbed by Lucius Septimus, who had once served under him, the renowned Roman general died in full view of his wife, who was watching from aboard the ship that carried them from Greece to Egypt.

Greece to continue the fight from there. The odds were growing longer, however. In desperate need of military and financial aid, Pompey sent one of his sons to Egypt to ask for help. Cleopatra had vanished by then from Alexandria, but the regency council received young Pompey cordially—and generously: He was given supplies of grain, along with five hundred Gabinian soldiers and sixty ships. In gratitude, the part of the Senate that had followed Pompey to Greece issued a decree naming their leader guardian of Egypt's young king.

It was something of a hollow gesture, since Ptolemy's new protector was himself in great danger. From Italy, Caesar successfully invaded Spain, routed Pompey's partisans there, then pursued the enemy to Greece. The decisive battle was fought in August of 48 B.C. at Pharsalus in Thessaly. Caesar won overwhelmingly. He was now master of Rome, the most powerful man in the world.

Pompey had escaped with his life, however, and he sped to Egypt, hoping to raise new armies and resume the fight. In September, the last month of the Egyptian year, he sailed with a small contingent of ships toward the shore at Pelusium, near Egypt's eastern border.

As he approached, a small boat rowed out to meet him. In it were three men: Achillas, a Hellenized Egyptian who was a general in Ptolemy's army, and two Gabinian officers. One of these, Lucius Septimus, had served under Pompey in former days. Assuming they were there to welcome him, Pompey, accompanied by only four of his attendants, stepped aboard the little boat. By the time he reached the shore he was dead, stabbed by Septimus.

The reason for this treachery toward a friend of Egypt and the avowed guardian of its king was coldly practical: Pothinus, the ever-scheming leader of the regency council, had advised Ptolemy that the murder was the best way to ensure that Romans of any political stripe would leave Egypt alone. Caesar would surely pursue Pompey, the reasoning went, and if he found him dead, he'd have no reason to stay. Besides, Pothinus concluded, Caesar might even show himself grateful to Egypt for killing his enemy.

Pompey sailed to Pelusium rather than Alexandria because King Ptolemy and his army were nearby, encamped in the shadow of Mount Casius, preparing to do battle with Cleopatra. Like her father before her, Cleopatra had no intention of accepting exile as her final fate.

Some scholars believe that when she was forced out of Alexandria, the queen had originally sought refuge in Upper Egypt, where she had considerable support. Others hold that there could have been no safe haven for her anywhere in Egypt, and she left the country immediately. In any case, Cleopatra eventually made her way to the Philistine city-state of Ashkelon, which lay between Egypt and Palestine. Some years before, her grandfather had saved Ashkelon from being taken over by Judea. For that, the city revered him, and Auletes after him, and it welcomed Cleopatra now.

She had not fled Alexandria empty-handed by any means. Her money and jewels were ample to raise a mercenary army. From her base in Ashkelon, she enlisted soldiers from among the Arab tribesmen in the neighboring kingdom of Nabatea. They were, on the whole, a motley lot to pit against the seasoned Gabinians, who formed the core of Ptolemy's army, but they would have to do.

So it was that in 47 B.C., Cleopatra and her Arabs faced Ptolemy's forces about thirty miles east of Pelusium. For days, the two armies eyed each other from positions on either side of the border, but neither offered battle. It was as though each waited for the tide of larger world events to wash over Egypt's shores and decide the issue for them. Both were aware that Caesar was coming.

Inside her tent, Cleopatra must have given lengthy thought to what this might mean. Her few partisans back in Alexandria would have kept her informed on the progress of Rome's civil war. Now that there was a clear victor, he could dispose of Egypt as he liked. Caesar could finally make this richest of nations a Roman province; that would please the Senate, and he certainly had the military resources to do it. Or he could maintain Egypt's current status as a vassal state of Rome—but an independent one. If he chose the latter course, whom would he back as ruler?

He had no reason to prefer Ptolemy; after all, the regency council had backed Pompey in the war. On the other hand, Caesar was famous for forgiving his former enemies. This curious trait would surely have puzzled Cleopatra, since the Ptolemies had always considered vengeance a natural perquisite and pleasure of kingship. Still, she would have been aware of it, and much else besides: She had kept up with the affairs of Rome, since the superpower to the west was vital to her survival. She could hardly have failed to realize that its new ruler was a many-faceted man.

In his youth, Caesar had been regarded by other important figures in Rome as bright and amiable, but something of a fop—not serious enough to become a threat. Only a few saw at first the relentless ambition that lay at his core. As he rose militarily and politically, however, Caesar's true nature became clearer. He was deemed to be a gifted writer, and something of an intellectual. Cleopatra herself had not read any of his work (Latin was not among her several languages), but scholars at the Library had probably described to her his prose: incisive and unadorned, the work of a man who knew his own power and felt no need for embellishment.

Many times over, Caesar had proved himself in war. He was thought by many to be the greatest general since Alexander, a strategic genius who moved his legions at breakneck speed to surprise and overwhelm his enemies. And, like Alexander, he was worshiped by his men. During campaigns he lived as they did, sharing their hardships and dangers and enjoying no special privileges. It was said that his troops would follow him across the River Styx if he ordered an attack on Hades.

Even so, they made up bawdy songs about him—apparently as a sign of affection. A typical example was the tune that became popular

A portrait bust of Julius Caesar, circa 1st century B.C., *below*. Opposite page: The Landing of Julius Caesar depicts Caesar leading his troops in battle. Part of Caesar's military genius was his ability to inspire his men to exceed their own normal limits. "He was so much master of the good-will and hearty service of his soldiers," wrote the Greek biographer Plutarch, "that those who in other expeditions were but ordinary men, displayed a courage past defeating or with-standing when they went upon any danger where Caesar's glory was concerned."

after his conquests in Gaul:

Home we bring our bald whoremaster:
Romans! Lock your wives away!
All those bags of gold you sent him
Went his Gallic tarts to pay.

Reportedly, Caesar wasn't offended by these ditties; on the contrary, he found them quite amusing—except, perhaps, the part about the baldness. The Julian clan, to which he belonged, claimed descent from the goddess Venus, and they were known for being a rather handsome people. Caesar was said to be sensitive about his thinning hair.

Evidently, however, the middle-aged, thrice-married general was not sensitive about his reputation as a prodigious philanderer, which was well deserved. He had slept with queens (kings too, some said), along with uncounted lesser mortals. By all reports, Caesar was as formidable in bed as in battle.

What exactly did Cleopatra make of his womanizing? Chronicles of the times do not say, but it is easy to envision her sitting in her sun-baked desert tent and pondering the matter, wondering if his susceptibility to feminine allure might work in her favor. But how to exploit it? Egyptian women were famous for their sexual artistry, and Cleopatra had probably brought the same curiosity to this subject as she had to arithmetic or astronomy. But whatever she knew, she probably knew only in theory. History provides no evidence whatever that at this point in her life, the queen was anything but a virgin.

What, then, if in her inexperience she failed to please this connoisseur of women? One can almost hear her thinking the problem through: If Caesar did try to seduce her, she would probably do well to feign great pleasure in the act of love. Well, she could certainly pretend—and doubtless she'd have to: She was only twenty-one, and he was more than thirty years older. The prospect of sleeping with him couldn't have been appetizing.

Still, her fate, and Egypt's, depended on Caesar's whim. She would do what she had to.

The real question was how to get to him alive. Probably he was already in residence in the royal compound, but the palace was held by her brother's minions, who could be counted on to kill her on sight.

So how could she reach him? She would have spent long hours thinking about that. Finally, Cleopatra settled on a plan that combined comparative safety with maximum drama and wit. She was about to prove, and not for the last time, that she was a woman who knew how to make an entrance.

⚱

The exiled queen was right in assuming that Caesar was already in Alexandria. He had arrived with ten warships and a small fighting force of thirty-two hundred infantry and eight hundred cavalry. To the anger and dismay of the city's citizens, he strode to the palace accompanied by a twelve-man consular guard bearing official Roman insignia. This entrance looked altogether too military to the nationalist-minded Alexandrians, and they rioted for several days, killing several of his soldiers. The deaths were unfortunate, but the general probably wasn't overly perturbed. Discontent among the rabble was nothing new, and—consummate politician that he was—he knew how to deal with it.

He addressed the populace personally, reminding the people that in the past he had supported Egypt's independence, and assuring them that as a representative of Roman law, he was there to restore the peace and stability of the realm. Whether anyone believed him or not, his promises were sufficient for the moment. A wary quiet descended, and he was able to turn his attention to unsnarling the Oriental tangle of Egyptian politics.

At least he could review the problems in comfort. No doubt the palace was quite the most luxurious dwelling Caesar had ever seen—as a Roman would expect of the sybaritic Greeks. One can envision him

Caesar receives tribute from Egypt in this Renaissance fresco by Andrea del Sarto, *right*.
Previous spread: A conquering Julius Caesar holds the world in his outstretched hand in this 19th-century painting by French artist Adolphe Yvon, who was a favorite of Napoleon III. Caesar's vanquished foes are tethered to his horse. The white figures with scythes at the left of the painting symbolize death, and the flying figure behind Caesar is probably a metaphor for conquest.

lying back in one of its vast, porphyry baths, reflecting on how pleasant it was to be there after the long years in hostile Gaul and the rigors of the civil war. The Alexandrians were a contentious lot, but what a city this was, with its wealth, its sophisticated Hellenism, its echoes of Egyptian antiquity. It must have appealed to both his intellect and his senses.

No doubt it also called to his ambition. In this city was the tomb of the great Alexander. Caesar visited it, probably regarding the gilded corpse with both reverence and a degree of envy, since this long-dead Macedonian was the paradigm for all conquerors. But there were differences: Alexander had ruled unchallenged and absolutely; Caesar was merely the foremost man in a republic. Nominally, at least, he still relied on the goodwill of the Roman Senate. But, as his enemies in Rome suspected and feared, he hoped to eliminate that inconvenience.

It would take time, a precious commodity to the general. Alexander had been young—only thirty-three—when he died, having by then brought the whole known world under his sway. Caesar was fifty-two, and as yet he was far from rivaling Alexander, in extent of territory or control of it. There must have been many moments when the scarred and war-weary Roman felt the weight of his years, as he marked the distance still to cross before absolute power lay within his grasp.

Caesar's first few days in Alexandria would have stirred such shadowed moods, despite the attractions of the city. The civil war had given him victory over Pompey, but his enemy's ignominious death had robbed that triumph of much of its luster. And now, after the fairly straightforward business of battle, he faced the tedium of sorting out Egypt's problem: What to do with this latest generation of Macedonians, the current Ptolemies; how to bring these errant, squabbling children into line.

Not long after he settled himself in the palace, Caesar sent for both Cleopatra and Ptolemy. The young king returned promptly

Cleopatra presents herself to Caesar in this nineteenth-century engraving of a painting by J. L. Gerome. At the queen's feet is Apollodorus, who smuggled her into the palace.

Most ancient historians agree that Cleopatra was carried to Caesar concealed in a rug, but Plutarch, the Greek biographer who gives the most reliable account of her, describes the covering as a bedspread.

"She took a small boat, and in the dusk of the evening landed near the palace. She was at a loss how to get in undiscovered, till she thought of putting herself into the coverlet of a bed and lying at length, whilst Apollodorus tied up the bedding and carried it on his back through the gates to Caesar's apartment. Caesar was first captivated by this proof of Cleopatra's bold wit, and was afterwards so overcome by the charm of her society, that he made a reconciliation between her and her brother, on condition that she should rule as his colleague in the kingdom."

from his desert encampment along with his advisors, including the eunuch Pothinus. The Roman general dealt with them cordially, but there was loathing behind his smiles, for a minion of Ptolemy had recently presented him with the embalmed head of Pompey, holding the grisly thing up before him with simpering pride, as though he should be pleased. Losing his composure for once, Caesar had wept with rage. Pompey had been his enemy, but a worthy one, deserving an honorable death in battle, not murder at the hands of perfidious foreigners. Such a deed could not go unpunished.

Meanwhile, he awaited Cleopatra.

His informers in Egypt would have told him a great deal about the deposed young queen, prompting at the very least some idle curiosity. They would have remarked on how brilliant she was—willful and determined, but charming nonetheless, a poised and gifted conversationalist. Certainly they would have described her voice, low-pitched and musical. Every listener was struck by it, even more than by her appearance.

Knowing the danger she faced in attempting to reach the palace, he must have wondered how she would manage it, or if she would manage it at all.

Given the circumstances and the characters involved, the first meeting of Caesar and Cleopatra is surely one of history's most extraordinary encounters.

Caesar was alone in his quarters late at night when a visitor was announced, a merchant bearing a gift. The man was admitted, a tall, strapping fellow with a rug slung over his shoulder. When it was unrolled, Cleopatra tumbled out.

History leaves the rest of the evening largely to the imagination, but presumably it began with some polite, mutual assessment. No doubt Caesar was surprised by Cleopatra's entrance, and he probably

Bronze aegises, such as this one with the bust of Isis, were used for protection by priestesses during adoration rituals.

also found it amusing and admirable: It showed spirit and wit. Doubtless, too, he found her attractive; men invariably did.

Cleopatra's beauty was unconventional. The high-bridged nose of the Ptolemies was a little too long in her case to fit the Roman ideal, and there were other flaws. In a time when fair complexions were admired, she was rather dark, perhaps reflecting a heritage from one of her grandmothers, a Seleucid princess with some Persian blood. But her hair was lovely—luxuriant, and coppery in color. And there was something indefinably compelling about her face; it shone with intelligence and strength of will.

As for her, she must have been attracted instantly by the one quality that she admired most and that Caesar had in such abundance: power. In his presence, she would have seen that it resided not just in his rank but in his person, explaining why his armies gladly followed him and his enemies feared him.

They surely found much to talk about, this unique and brilliant pair. Caesar probably told Cleopatra what he'd already told Ptolemy and Pothinus officially: He was in Egypt to keep Rome's promise to enforce the terms of Auletes' will. The late king had wished for her and Ptolemy to rule jointly, and that was the way it would be. Perhaps he pointed out that a shared throne was better than no throne at all—a point which, as an exile, Cleopatra would have found easy enough to grasp. For the moment, it might indeed be politic to share.

Whatever they discussed, there came a time when the talking stopped. In the course of that first night, they became lovers.

Her Roman critics would later say that Cleopatra's motives were wholly political. But the course that her life took after this first meeting suggests otherwise. She had met a man with the genius to teach her and with the power to protect her—the power, in fact, to realize her dreams for herself and Egypt. Caesar was the only equal she would ever know. She was in love with him, as she would never be again.

Chapter IV
DEATH OF THE DREAM

The next morning, Caesar invited Ptolemy to attend him, and the thirteen-year-old monarch arrived to meet with a most unpleasant shock: Not only was his hated sister back in the palace, but she and the new master of the world were clearly on very intimate terms.

In response, the king of Egypt threw a tantrum. He ran out of the room, screaming to his supporters that he'd been betrayed. Rushing into the streets, he quickly gathered a crowd. He tore the royal diadem from his head and flung it to the ground, exhorting the people to take his side against Cleopatra and her Roman lover.

The dramatic appeal was effective, in part because Pothinus had already seeded Alexandria with rumors that Caesar's intention in coming to Egypt had always been to install the pro-Roman Cleopatra as sole ruler. Caesar's soldiers succeeded in dragging Ptolemy back into the palace, but the damage was done. A furious mob followed in their wake, quieting only when Caesar himself emerged to promise the protesters that they would be satisfied with his disposition of the matter.

That disposition was announced a few days later at a lavish banquet: Ptolemy and Cleopatra—brother and sister, husband and wife—had reconciled and would rule Egypt jointly, as their father had wished. To sweeten the deal, Caesar declared that the island of Cyprus, annexed by Rome a decade earlier, would be returned to the Ptolemies. Its new king and queen would be Auletes' youngest children, eleven-year-old Ptolemy XIV and his sister Arsinoë, who was now about eighteen.

The news was enough to dampen dissent

The great French actress Sarah Bernhardt is attired for the role of Cleopatra in this 19th-century painting by Georges Clairin.

in Alexandria for the time being, but the peace was fragile—and the mix inside the royal compound was volatile. Caesar had decided that Arsinoë and the younger Ptolemy should delay taking their thrones in Cyprus until stability returned to Alexandria (ostensibly so he could protect them, more likely so he could keep an eye on them). As a result, four royal Ptolemies and their entourages were living in close quarters. It couldn't have been comfortable. Cleopatra despised her brother-husband and her sister Arsinoë, and they both hated her. The city, meanwhile, seethed with resentment at the presence of Caesar, fearing that his liaison with Cleopatra might foreshadow the end of Egypt's independence.

The tensions soon flared into open war. At the end of October 48 B.C., about two and a half months after his arrival in Alexandria, Caesar learned that Pothinus had secretly ordered Ptolemy's army back from its desert encampment on Egypt's eastern border. Led by the general Achillas, a force of twenty thousand infantry and two thousand cavalry was marching toward the capital. Not only did this force outnumber Caesar's troops five to one, but most of nationalistic Alexandria could be counted on to rise in Ptolemy's support once the army reached the city.

Caesar put Ptolemy under house arrest, hoping to prevent the young king from becoming the rallying point for Cleopatra's enemies. At the same time, the Roman commander sent envoys to summon reinforcements from Rome's territories in the Levant.

In late November, Achillas attacked the royal compound. Caesar's troops repelled the assault amid vicious street fighting, but a greater danger was at hand. Achillas was trying to seize the seventy-two royal Egyptian ships in Alexandria's harbor. If he had them under his control, he could cut Caesar off from supplies and reinforcements arriving by sea.

The Roman soldiers blocked the effort to take the fleet, but Caesar, realizing he probably couldn't hold the ships for long against superior numbers, decided to burn them. The fire spread to the docks and destroyed a warehouse holding a large consignment of

The portrait of Cleopatra on this gold coin, *right,* shows the queen with a simple Greek hairstyle. The words on the coin are Greek for "Cleopatra" and "Queen."

scrolls that were either on their way to or from the great Library. Nevertheless, the harbor was now in Caesar's hands, and on the same day the Egyptian ships were torched, he secured his position with a daring raid that captured the Pharos lighthouse.

All this Cleopatra must have watched in a state of heart-clutching anxiety from a window in her palace. Caesar was her lover by night and her champion by day, and as both woman and queen, her fate depended on his. And that fate was still uncertain. The queen's partisans suffered a setback when Arsinoë stole out of the palace one night and fled to Achillas. Applauding her defiance, Alexandrians and the army hailed her as the true queen.

Before long, however, Achillas had cause to regret Arsinoë's escape. The princess had brought along her chief advisor, the eunuch Ganymedes, who challenged the general's power. Rival factions arose within the army.

Back at the royal compound, Pothinus learned of the squabbling between Achillas and Ganymedes and dispatched messengers to the general, promising his continued support and probably also vowing to slip out of the palace himself, with Ptolemy, as soon as possible; the young king's presence with the army would assure Achillas' control. But Caesar intercepted the messengers, uncovered Pothinus' plans, and had the eunuch killed. No doubt the execution afforded him considerable satisfaction: One of Pompey's murderers had been dealt with, and Alexandria's most dangerous anti-Roman political leader was now out of the way.

The most effective anti-Roman military leader was soon to follow: Achillas lost his power struggle with Ganymedes and was put to death. Any comfort that this gave Caesar's legionaries was short-lived, however, for Ganymedes proved a crafty and capable general himself. He brought in a new fleet, laid siege to the royal compound, and pumped seawater into the wells that fed the palace. Caesar's troops, famed for their engineering prowess, countered the sabotage by digging new wells overnight. Day after day the fighting went on, with neither side gaining a clear advantage.

THE NILE

The Nile is the longest river in the world, running 4,187 miles from its most remote headstream. It begins at Khartoum in Sudan at the juncture of its two main tributaries, the Blue Nile, coming out of North Ethiopia, and the White Nile, from Lake Victoria. Drawing water from the large lakes of East Africa and the Ethiopian highlands, it snakes its way through southern Egypt, or Upper Egypt, shrinking and swelling with the seasonal rains until it reaches the rich delta, where it empties into the Mediterranean.

Along its banks multitudes of wildlife thrive, and fields of cotton, corn, flax, and rice flourish. The early Egyptians, having a substantial knowledge of the biological sciences, made naturalistic drawings and carvings of most of the indigenous plants and animals that lived within this region, as well as those they imported. Their art

recorded ibis, herons, falcons, hawks, and eagles. Even lions, elephants, and hippopotami, animals that no longer inhabit this region, were immortalized in their effigies.

The land around the Nile is rich in metals and minerals: gypsum, limestone, alabaster, quartzite, granite, gold, iron, copper, and tin. These materials, still mined today, were crafted into artifacts, pyramids, and palaces. The Egyptians classified the raw materials and used them according to their inherent properties: Obelisks were made from the granite, while the hardest of stones, used for most of the buildings, came from the Nubian desert. Still standing today are the ruins of several of those structures, such as the temples at Dendera, Luxor, and the temple at Philae, which sits on an island in the Nile. Like jewels themselves, these sites testify to the vanished grandeur of ancient Egypt.

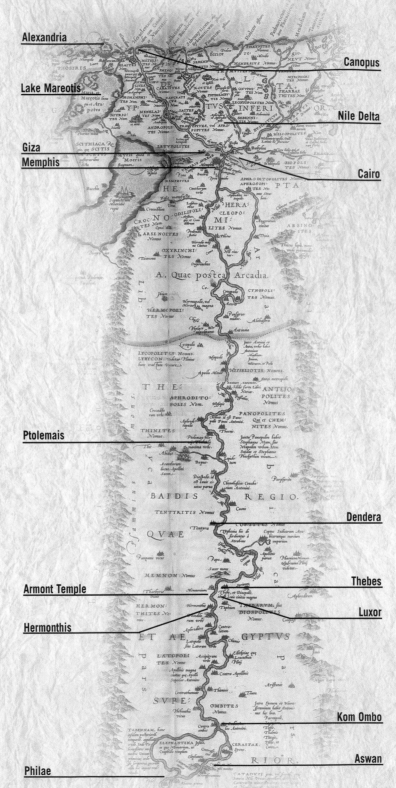

At this point, Caesar took one of the strategic gambles that had so often marked his career: He released Ptolemy from house arrest and sent him out to Ganymedes' army. The publicly stated reason was that the young king could help restore order. More likely, Caesar was wagering that Ptolemy and Arsinoë, with a kingdom at stake, would behave the way Ptolemaic siblings usually did: They'd be at each other's throats.

Cleopatra and Caesar enjoy their voyage up the Nile, *following spread.* In the print of a 19th-century painting by Henri-Pierre Picou, the artist conveys something of their ship's majesty, if not its scale. It would have been much larger, big enough to accommodate a sumptuous sleeping chamber and dining hall, and probably even a temple.

If that was Caesar's hope, it was soon dashed. Arsinoë ceded to her brother uncontested leadership of the army, and Ganymedes vanished from the scene. But a far more important military development was now in the works: Caesar's call for reinforcements was about to be answered. Early in March of 47 B.C., a fleet carrying Syrian, Asian, and Arabian troops under the command of a Graeco-Persian named Mithridates approached Egypt's eastern frontier.

The relief force joined up at Ashkelon with a contingent of Jewish warriors from Judea, and the combined army easily took the fortress of Pelusium on Egypt's eastern border. Instead of proceeding directly west toward Alexandria across the widest part of the Nile delta, however, the army marched south, then back to the northwest toward the capital. The reason would soon become clear.

Near Lake Mareotis, Mithridates' army was met by a much larger force, led by King Ptolemy himself. The relief army appeared to be doomed—but appearances deceived. Caesar, leaving only a small garrison in Alexandria to protect Cleopatra, was marching his own troops at high speed to link up with Mithridates.

On March 27, 47 B.C., Ptolemy's army was caught in a classic pincer movement and routed. Panicked Egyptian soldiers ran for their camp. Caesar promptly stormed it, and a slaughter ensued. In all the carnage, however, the young king was nowhere to be found.

Later that day, Caesar received word that Ptolemy had fled to the Nile and attempted to escape by boat. The vessel, overburdened with other escapees, sank, and the king reportedly drowned. Meanwhile, his sister Arsinoë, so briefly a queen, had been captured. Plans were made to transport her to Rome as a trophy of war.

That night, Caesar marched back to Alexandria in triumph, his return marking the first time the city had ever fallen to a foreign enemy. He may have expected mixed fury and despair from the populace, but with typical Greek pragmatism, the Alexandrians sided with the winner, rushing out to greet the Roman conqueror with statues of their gods.

Caesar's victory was not as yet complete, however. Ancient legend had it that drowning in the Nile conferred instant rebirth and immortality. This widely held belief invited would-be usurpers, pretending to be the reincarnated Ptolemy, to challenge Cleopatra's power. Caesar therefore ordered the Nile dredged. The king's body, quite definitively dead, was retrieved and his golden armor displayed before the people. With that, the brief, bloody Alexandrian War was over.

For Cleopatra, this must have been a time of singular happiness, qualified only by Caesar's mandate—issued for reasons of domestic peace—that she share her throne with her surviving half-brother, eleven-year-old Ptolemy XIV. But the arrangement was only nominal; for all practical purposes, she ruled alone. And these days had brought another, even greater gift—a surer harbinger of her future glory, and Egypt's. She was pregnant.

Despite his consort's condition, Caesar had every reason to leave Egypt once the Alexandrian War was over. His business there was done. He had come seeking Pompey, and to collect on Auletes' old debt, and to end Egypt's civil strife. Now Pompey was dead, Caesar's liaison with Cleopatra assured him of whatever financial assistance he might ever need from Egypt, and the brief civil war had left the queen secure on her throne. Besides, he had business elsewhere. The political situation in Rome remained volatile, and Pompey's sons and supporters had raised a new army

in northern Africa that he would have to deal with sooner or later. Moreover, there was a threatened uprising against Rome in the province of Pontus. Yet Caesar stayed, as if unable to separate himself from the young queen who had so enchanted him.

Cleopatra made the most of his presence. Accompanied by four hundred Egyptian ships, many of them carrying troops, Caesar and Cleopatra journeyed up the Nile the entire length of Egypt, a trip that was at once a victory celebration, a tour, a political mission, and a honeymoon.

They traveled aboard Cleopatra's state barge, a floating palace of cedar and cypress that was probably some three hundred feet long, fitted out with gardens and columned walkways, a dining hall, and even shrines to the gods. The first stop was Giza, where Caesar was doubtless as awed as any other tourist by the great pyramids and the sphinx; Romans, comparative newcomers on the world scene, were invariably impressed by antiquities, and these monuments dated back two and a half millennia. From Giza it was a day's sail to the old capital of Memphis, where, at the necropolis at nearby Saqqara, the master of the Roman world must have seen his first mummy.

On either side of the river as they continued to float southward lay golden fields of wheat and barley, the basis of the nation's wealth. This—not the Greek city of Alexandria—was the real Egypt. After about a week they reached Thebes and the massive splendor of the Luxor and Karnak temples, and a bit farther on was Hermonthis, where, four eventful years earlier, the teenaged Queen Cleopatra had presided over the installation of the sacred Buchis bull. Perhaps it was now that she decided that if her child was a son, she would build a shrine

Mummification continued to be widely practiced throughout Egypt, including Alexandria, during the Ptolemaic period. Those who were wealthy could afford elaborate coffins, sometimes as many as three of them enclosing a single mummy. Below is the innermost coffin, circa 250 B.C., of a man named Djeho, son of Psammetichus. *Right:* The eternally mysterious Great Sphinx of Giza stands before one of the pyramids. Carved from an outcrop of rock around 2550 B.C., it is Egypt's oldest surviving sphinx.

here to celebrate his birth.

The royal journey ended at Aswan. Here, at Egypt's southern frontier, was the lovely island temple of Philae, sacred to Isis and built by earlier Ptolemies. At Philae, as elsewhere along the route, Cleopatra would have been greeted with joy as the goddess incarnate. Caesar, her consort, would have been hailed as the embodiment of the great god Amon.

Doubtless the Nile journey was useful in consolidating Cleopatra's power; it was good for the majority of her subjects, the native Egyptians, to see their queen again—and to see in Caesar and his Roman troops the awesome power that stood behind her throne. But to Cleopatra, the trip must have been necessary in a subtler but even more vital way. Egyptian custom had no wedding ceremony as such; a man and woman who presented themselves as a couple were merely accepted as a married pair. In showing herself to all Egypt in the company of Caesar, she was affirming that she was not just his mistress but his wife, her nominal union with her much-younger brother notwithstanding.

Cleopatra understood perfectly well that Caesar had a wife in Rome and that, in any case, Roman law did not recognize marriage between a Roman and a foreigner. But it must have been essential to her that here in her own land, at least, her liaison with Caesar was accepted as legitimate—because she loved him, of course, but also because of her child. Impending motherhood had brought with it new dreams. If she gave birth to a son, he might have a claim to be master not only of Egypt but of Rome as well. Roman legalities would have to bend to allow it, but he could hope to rule an empire unmatched in all history.

THE TEMPLE AT DENDERA

The temple complex of Hathor at Dendera was begun by the last native Egyptian dynasty, the 30th. It has a long history of reconditioning with additions made during the Ptolemaic and Roman periods. It was largely completed by Ptolemy II, and several subsequent Ptolemies added to it and decorated it. By Cleopatra's time, the only area left for her to adorn was the main temple's rear, or south, wall. The Dendera complex has two birth houses (structures built to mark the divine birth of royal children), a Coptic basilica, a sanatorium, a sacred lake, and a temple to Isis.

(A) The Hypostyle Hall is an extraordinary hall with a facade enclosed by a screen wall supporting the ceiling with square capitals carved to resemble kind Hathor's face. On the interior walls a king is shown wearing the crowns of Upper and Lower Egypt.

(B) The Hall of Appearances was built by the Ptolemies. It is surrounded by six rooms: **(1)** the treasury room, holding holy objects made of metal; **(2)** a room to store incense and perfumes; **(3)** the Nile Chamber, an exit for priests bringing in water; **(4)** a smaller room the priests used as a passageway; **(5)** a storage chamber; and **(6)** a room that served as an outside exit that allowed food and drink to be brought in for festivals.

(C) The Hall of Offerings is where priests laid out offerings for the gods. It is actually the entrance to the temple and is lighted only by four ceiling vents. Inside there is a small chapel used for sacrificial offerings.

(D) The Hall of the Ennead contains statues of gods and kings who partook in the ceremonies held at the temple. The south wall of the hall is inscribed with the texts of the Hymns of Awakening.

(E) The Sanctuary, housing statues of Hathor, her *barque* or sacred ritual boat, and Horus, beautifully depicts the awakening, bathing, anointing, and feeding of the goddess Hathor.

(F) The Astronomical Ceiling is exquisitely decorated with images of vultures and winged disks. Symbolic representations of the north and south portions of the sky depict the hours of the day and night as well as the regions of the moon and sun. The bays to the right show the northern stars, and the left bays show the southern stars. The solar cycle is represented by the sky goddess Nut, who was thought to give birth to the sun at the beginning of each day.

Below: **Cleopatra and Caesarion make offerings to the gods in a detail from the south wall of the Temple of Hathor at Dendera. The queen, at the far left, wears the horns-and-disk headdress of Hathor. Her son, in front of her, wears the double crown of Upper and Lower Egypt, embellished by the ram's horns of the god Amon. Receiving their offerings are Hathor and, in front of her, a minor god, Ihi.**

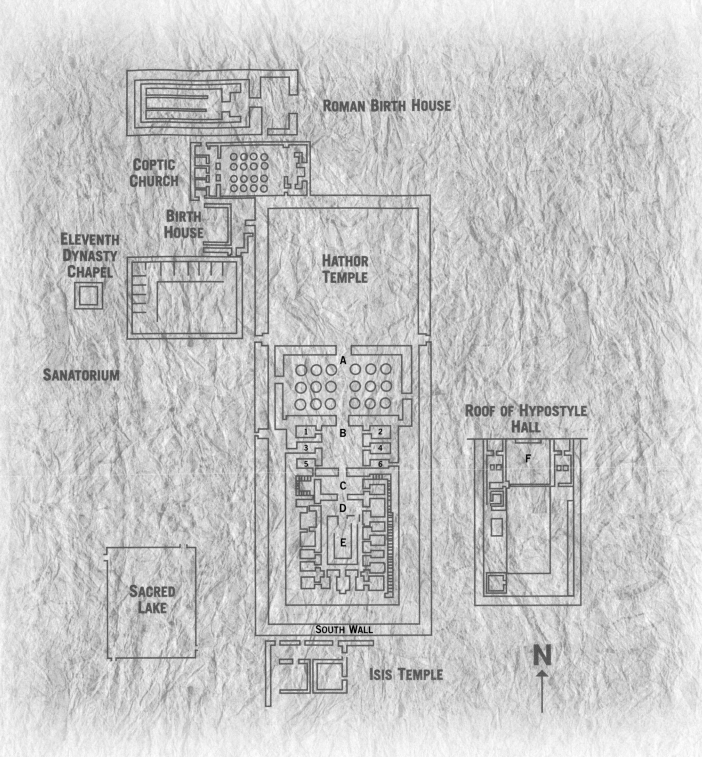

Roman Birth House

Coptic
Church

Birth
House

Eleventh
Dynasty
Chapel

Hathor
Temple

Sanatorium

A

B

Roof of Hypostyle
Hall

1   2
3   4
5   6

C

D

E

F

Sacred
Lake

South Wall

Isis Temple

N

E ven in ruins, the Temple of Karnak retains something of its ancient majesty. Home to Amon, the ruler god of Upper Egypt, Karnak was the largest house of worship ever built for any deity of any religion. Its central sanctuary was so vast that St. Peter's Basilica and the cathedrals of Milan and Notre Dame would have easily fit inside it. Begun some four thousand years ago, the temple was expanded and embellished over a period of two thousand years.

Above: A view across the sacred lake at the remains of a gateway at Karnak.

In showing Caesar her country, Cleopatra was laying before him a dowry of stupendous richness. And almost certainly, she was mustering all her charm to make him complicit in her vision: Egypt's wealth and Rome's might, East and West united, a world ruled by the two of them, and after them by their son. She was showing him, as they walked among her people, what it meant to hold absolute power, to be a god on earth.

Possibly he was tempted by her vision, but Caesar was much older and far more aware of the realities of the wider world—the fractious, mercurial politics of the Romans, their mistrust of ambition, their republican distaste for kings, the unlikelihood that they would endure any sort of monarch, the utter impossibility of their accepting a woman and a foreigner as their ruler, or even as the consort of their ruler.

Cleopatra's hard, clear ambition may well have endeared her to him all the more. Along with loving her as a woman and admiring her as a queen of ancient lineage, Caesar must have seen in Cleopatra a younger version of himself, possessing the same appetite and drive, not yet sullied by compromise and cynicism. Still, he couldn't match her faith in a conjoined future, any more than he could match the extent of her love. For him, it was too late for that. She loved him, it seems, with the passion a woman brings only to her first love. He loved her merely with the poignance that a man brings to his last.

☷

In June of 47 B.C., soon after their river journey reached its end, Caesar left Cleopatra. Only days later, Cleopatra gave birth to a healthy son. She named him

This statue of a pharaoh from the Temple of Karnak, *below,* illustrates the Egyptian artistic device of hierarchical proportions; that is, the size of a statue denotes the importance of the subject. Thus the pharaoh's wife, in front of him, is much smaller than he.

Ptolemy Caesar, stressing his paternity, but the people of Alexandria gave him the nickname he would always be known by: Caesarion—"Caesar's son," or "little Caesar." Her love for him would be all-consuming—because he was her son, because he was Caesar's, and because he was the vessel of the imperial future she aspired to. She celebrated his birth by issuing a coin showing the two of them depicted as Isis suckling the infant Horus, the goddess and her royal son.

The boy was scarcely more than a month old when his absent father put down the insurrection in Pontus with such speed that he famously adapted a Greek epigram to describe it to his Latin-speaking readers: *Veni, vidi, vici*—"I came, I saw, I conquered." Then he returned to Italy briefly before setting out for north Africa to contend with the large army raised by Pompey's partisans there. He vanquished it on April 6, 46 B.C., and two and a half months later he was back in Rome, preparing to reap the glory of his conquests.

Triumphs decreed by the Senate for Rome's victorious generals were always elaborate affairs, featuring parades that displayed booty and prisoners from the conquered lands. The prisoners were usually killed later, while Rome's citizens celebrated with public feasting and lavish ceremonies and games, all financed by the honoree. Caesar's triumphs were especially spectacular; he had always known how to court popular favor.

Between September 20 and October 1 he celebrated four triumphs, commemorating victories in Gaul, Egypt, Pontus, and north Africa. The Egyptian triumph was the second of the four, and its parade included a model of the Pharos lighthouse and huge paintings depicting the deaths of Pothinus and Achillas. There were heaps of treasure—gifts from Cleopatra—and an assortment of animals, including a giraffe, the first the Romans had ever seen.

The crowds were delighted with all this, but their enthusiasm cooled when they saw the procession's climactic exhibit, young princess Arsinoë IV, draped in chains, marching at the head of the Egyptian prisoners. She walked with her head high, bearing the chains as though they were jewels, showing only contempt for her captors. The throng grew silent, then began grumbling. Something about her—her youth and beauty, or her defiant pride—had touched them. Sensing the mood, Caesar decided to let her live. She would be sent to the sanctuary of Artemis at Ephesus.

Soon after the triumphs, Cleopatra herself arrived in Rome, along with her brother, her infant son, and an entourage large enough to proclaim her status as queen of the wealthiest nation on earth. The ostensible purpose of the visit was to have Rome renew the alliance it had made with her father, but she also had other aims in mind, chiefly a reunion with Caesar. Probably, too, she hoped that he would make some acknowledgment of Caesarion. Even though the boy could have no legal standing in Rome as Caesar's heir, she must have believed that a confirmation of his august parentage would carry weight with the people, and perhaps even with the Senate. Indeed, she may have thought that by now Caesar could dispose of such matters however he wished. The Senate had declared him dictator and consul for a term of ten years, confirming in law what already existed in fact: He was the ultimate power in Rome.

Caesar received Cleopatra with decorous cordiality; even had they not been lovers, it would have been proper for him to accord her the honors due a visiting head of state and to return the hospitality she had afforded him during his stay in Egypt. He installed her in his

handsome country estate across the Tiber from the city. She would live there for two years.

History records very little of this important time in Cleopatra's life; perhaps the notable Romans who paid court to her to curry favor with Caesar found it prudent to keep quiet about it later. Evidently, however, she initially struck most of the Romans who met her as quite the most glamorous visitor they had ever seen. She entertained lavishly, presiding over a salon of artists and intellectuals. For guests who didn't speak Greek (the more educated Romans usually did), she almost certainly would have mastered enough Latin to converse in her usual compelling way. And, like her father before her, she probably distributed generous bribes to any Romans powerful enough to be of use to her.

Caesar was busy with affairs of state and with a number of ambitious plans for improving Rome, but he must have spent as much private time with her as he could; and he would have entertained her publicly from time to time, introducing her to the city's aristocracy and intelligentsia. She probably renewed her acquaintance with his partisan Mark Antony, whom she had first met when he was a cavalry officer in his late twenties and she was a princess of fourteen. Perhaps she also encountered Caesar's great-nephew, seventeen-year-old Gaius Octavius, called Octavian, who was about to set off for the Adriatic town of Apollonia to finish his education. He was a slight, rather sickly youth, blond and very pale, with delicate features that made him striking—almost lovely rather than handsome. His intelligence was unmistakable.

father, but she also had other aims in mind, chiefly a reunion with Caesar. Probably, too, she hoped that he would make some acknowledgment of Caesarion. Even though the boy could have no legal standing in Rome as Caesar's heir, she must have believed that a confirmation of his august parentage would carry weight with the people, and perhaps even with the Senate. Indeed, she may have thought that by now Caesar could dispose of such matters however he wished. The Senate had declared him dictator and consul for a term of ten years, confirming in law what already existed in fact: He was the ultimate power in Rome.

Caesar received Cleopatra with decorous cordiality; even had they not been lovers, it would have been proper for him to accord her the honors due a visiting head of state and to return the hospitality she had afforded him during his stay in Egypt. He installed her in his

Closer to the Nile than any other temple, Kom Ombo was dedicated to, among other gods, Sobek, the fearsome crocodile god. Bejeweled sacred crocodiles were kept in pools here and were mummified after death. Kom Ombo, south of Luxor, was built by the Ptolemies, and some of its structures were erected by Ptolemy XII Auletes, Cleopatra's father. The capitals on the columns of the building depict open lotuses and open papyruses, thought symbolic of regeneration. Adorning the top of the building are two carvings of solar disks with cobras, symbols of royalty.

The Nile island of Philae is the subject of this 1871 lithograph of a Carl Werner painting. The columned structure to the right is Trajan's Kiosk, built more than a century after Cleopatra's death to honor a Roman emperor. The pylon on the left is the entrance to the Temple of Isis. The temple complex at Philae was considered to be among the most beautiful in Egypt. Near Aswan in southernmost Egypt, the island was also the site of a large statue of Ptolemy XII, Cleopatra's father.

It is not recorded whether Cleopatra ever met Calpurnia, Caesar's wife, or what the two thought of each other. Calpurnia could hardly have been unaware that the queen was her husband's mistress; all Rome knew it. But if she took Cleopatra's highly visible presence in the city as an insult, she probably bore it stoically, like the dignified Roman matron that she was. Caesar would have expected no less.

There was at least one gesture, however, that his legal wife must have found hard to endure. Soon after his triumphs and Cleopatra's arrival in Rome, Caesar celebrated the opening of his grand Forum Julium, a large annex he built to relieve the overcrowding of the Roman Forum. Its centerpiece was a splendid temple to Venus, Roman goddess of love, the patron deity of the Julian clan. A sculpture of the goddess stood inside it, and next to it Caesar had erected a second statue: a gilded image of Cleopatra.

The effigy of Egypt's queen spoke volumes. It did nothing to legitimize their liaison, but it proclaimed to the Roman world her singular importance to him. It also subtly accorded her the divine status she enjoyed in her homeland—and, by extension, it recognized the divinity of her child.

That unique honor was a dangerous one for Caesar to confer, and whatever admiration Cleopatra may have excited among the Romans began to wane. Ardent republicans grew especially hostile, viewing her as an affront to their very way of life. She was a foreigner, after all, Eastern and exotic, one of those luxury-smothered Hellenistic Greeks whose silken allure might corrupt even the sternest Roman. Furthermore, her power and independence were unseemly in a woman; queens, in fact, were unseemly. Governments should be run by men, as Rome's had always been. Worst of all, she was an autocrat. The Roman republic had no use for monarchs, had rejected them long ago. What insidious influence might a woman like this have over Caesar, in whose hands now rested the destiny of the entire Roman world?

In their suspicion of her, the republicans were not entirely wrong. As the daughter of a dynasty that had ruled absolutely for nearly three centuries, Cleopatra could scarcely have understood why great Caesar had to bother with a Senate that dared to place obstacles in his way and sometimes even criticized him openly. In Egypt, such dissent would be put down by force.

Perhaps she expressed such views to Caesar. In any event, he was showing more and more impatience with the Senate and the nobles. Reports began circulating that he planned to dismiss the Senate and declare himself king. Many people found these rumors extremely disturbing, but his popularity with the majority of Romans nonetheless seemed, for a time, limitless. He was the most successful general in Rome's history, a man who had vastly expanded the empire and enriched its capital. Most dissent remained muted, and in February of 44 B.C., the Senate declared him dictator for life. Total power was now within his grasp—and his enemies knew it.

Rome's annual February 14 festival, the Lupercalia, came shortly after Caesar's ascent to lifetime dictatorship, and it served as a sort of bellwether of public sentiment regarding that event. The Lupercalia was an ancient, rowdy festival in which a number of half-naked men ran through the streets carrying little whips with thongs called *februa* (after which February is named), striking revelers who crossed their paths. Women who wanted to have children made it a point to be hit, since the whips were supposed to confer fertility.

One wielder of the whip in the 44 B.C. festival was Mark Antony. As he approached the dais where Caesar sat watching the celebration, the muscular Antony leaped up on the platform and held a crown over the dictator's head.

BLOOD SPORT

Rome's infamous gladiatorial games began as a variation on Etruscan funeral rites, in which men died in mock combat to honor the deceased. At the first such event in Rome, in 264 B.C., slaves were forced to fight to the death as part of the funerals of several aristocrats.

Growing ever larger and more elaborate over the years, the games eventually came to include, along with mortal combat between armed men, the execution of helpless, unarmed criminals and political dissidents.

Patrons of the games also enjoyed watching the slaughter of animals. During the celebration of the opening of the Colosseum in A.D. 81, some five thousand creatures were killed in a single day.

Cleopatra may have attended a gladiatorial contest during her stay in Rome. If so, she was probably appalled. The Greeks, originators of the Olympic games, regarded sport as a celebration of the body and an honoring of the gods. Some of their contests did involve fighting, but they did not kill for sport.

Above: **Detail from a 3rd-century B.C. Italian fresco showing a gladiatorial duel.**

Left: **A Roman bronze figure of a gladiator, dating from 100 B.C. to A.D. 100.**

DREAMS AND PORTENTS

Had Caesar believed in signs and omens, he might have lived longer. According to legend, many evil portents preceded his death, among them, according to Plutarch, "the lights in the heavens, the noises heard in the night, and the wild birds which perched in the forum." And,

famously, the dictator had been warned by a soothsayer to "beware the Ides of March."

The morning of his last day, his wife, Calpurnia, told him she'd had terrible dreams during the night; weeping, she begged him not to go to the Senate. Caesar was alarmed,

says Plutarch, "for he never before discovered any womanish superstition in Calpurnia." He decided to heed her warning, but changed his mind when one of the conspirators against him, Decimus Brutus, hinted that the Senate planned that day to declare him

king of all the Roman provinces outside Italy.

Above: Calpurnia pleads with her husband to stay at home in this 18th-century Italian wall painting by Fabio Canal.

Caesar may have orchestrated the gesture himself; but if so, he cannot have been happy with its outcome. When he made a great show of refusing the crown, the crowd roared approval. Twice more Antony offered it, and twice more Caesar declined, each time to greater applause. The message was clear: However much Romans esteemed their leader, they wanted no king.

Nevertheless, Caesar was by now laying plans that promised to bring him greater glory. He was going to undertake the most sweeping military campaign of his career, a mission to avenge the Parthians' defeat of Crassus' army nine years earlier by conquering the entire Parthian empire. The expedition would be financed in part by Egyptian money, and Cleopatra was probably in on the planning of it. She intended to leave Rome when he did, staying close to him as long as possible to maintain her personal and political influence—and to ensure that Egypt, as Rome's ally, got its share of the spoils of war.

As for Caesar, he could hardly wait to be out of Rome. His republican critics were becoming more vocal and he less tolerant of them; after the complexities of politics, the comparative simplicity of battle would be a relief. He set a date for his departure: March 17, 44 B.C.

But he would never lead another army.

Some sixty republicans were plotting to kill him. Among their leaders were Lucius Cassius, an ambitious man who envied Caesar's power, and Marcus Brutus, whose motives were more complex.

Born into an old and honored family, Brutus was a dour moralist in the classic Roman mode—a model of rectitude and a fervent republican. He had backed Pompey over Caesar in the civil war, but Caesar had readily forgiven him. Indeed, Brutus was one of the dictator's great favorites, probably because Caesar believed (as did most of Rome) that he was Brutus' natural father. Brutus probably believed it too, but far from basking in his presumptive blood tie to the great man, he found the idea insupportable: It meant that his mother had betrayed his father and that he, the family-

proud Brutus, was a bastard.

On March 15, Brutus, Cassius, and several other conspirators surrounded Caesar as he approached the Senate and attacked him with daggers. Cassius slashed at his face, Brutus stabbed him in the groin, and the others joined in the slaughter. Caesar slumped down onto the pedestal of a statue of Pompey and bled to death from a multitude of wounds.

The master of Rome was gone, and with him Cleopatra's dream of world dominion. Gone was her lover, her friend and mentor, her confidant, protector and ally, the father of her child. One can only imagine the depth of her grief: For Cleopatra there were no more gods on earth.

☒

She had little time, however, to indulge her personal sorrow. Caesar's death had thrown the whole Roman world into turmoil. She had her son and her country to think about, and both were in peril.

Caesar had made a will a year before his death, and two days after his assassination, it was read to the Roman people. It named as Caesar's heir—and adopted son—his young great-nephew Octavian. No mention was made of Cleopatra or Caesarion, but if this disappointed the queen, it cannot have surprised her; she must have known that under the law, a Roman could not name a foreigner as heir.

The will effectively removed any quasi-legitimacy the queen may have enjoyed as Caesar's mistress, but her situation in Rome was not immediately precarious. Mark Antony, who had been consul with Caesar, was now the nominal head of state, and Cleopatra considered him a friend. Besides, many political observers felt that Antony was likely to end up as Caesar's long-term successor, since Octavian, only nineteen and still in school at Apollonia, was presumed to be much too young and inexperienced to reach for the reins of Roman government. Those who thought so had much to learn.

As soon as he heard of his uncle's death and will, Octavian set out for Rome to claim his inheritance—which, he reasoned, included leadership of the empire. Antony determined to oppose him, and once again Rome was catapulted into civil war.

Octavian's arrival on the scene made it imperative for Cleopatra to leave Rome: Caesar's legal heir would hardly look kindly on a woman who claimed that her son was the true heir by blood—or on the child himself. So by April of 44 B.C., the queen, her son, her brother, and her retinue had departed Rome for Alexandria.

She arrived home to a new set of troubles. Her ministers had directed the workings of Egypt's bureaucracy well enough, but Cleopatra's sister Arsinoë was making trouble from her sanctuary in Ephesus. The exiled princess, still coveting the throne, was supporting a pretender who claimed to be Ptolemy XIII, miraculously risen from the Nile. It must have occurred to the queen that Caesar should have killed the girl when he had the chance.

Cleopatra herself was evidently capable of such ruthlessness. Shortly after her return from Rome, her brother Ptolemy XIV died. Rumor said that the queen had poisoned him—and she probably had. He was fifteen at the time, old enough to challenge her power, as his older brother had done. Worse, he was a possible obstacle for Caesarion. Cleopatra could rule with only one co-regent, and it must be her son. That way, his succession would be assured, no matter what happened to her. So her brother had to die and her three-year-old child had to become king. It was the inexorable reasoning of the Ptolemies.

No less pressing than domestic matters was the course of the Roman war, since it could lead to eventual annexation of Egypt as a Roman province. At all costs, Cleopatra had to

It was the treachery of Brutus, who is depicted in this bust by Michelangelo, that finally overcame Caesar. Plutarch wrote that Caesar "fought and resisted" the other assassins, but "when he saw Brutus' sword drawn, he covered his face with his robes and submitted, letting himself fall . . ."

preserve her kingdom for herself and her son.

After the assassination, public sentiment had turned against the conspirators, and Brutus and Cassius had fled Italy in the summer of 44 B.C.—Brutus to Macedonia and Cassius to Syria. An army of republican supporters went with them. In Syria, Cassius faced an army led by a general who had been loyal to Caesar, Publius Cornelius Dolabella. The war was now on Egypt's doorstep, and both Dolabella and Cassius turned to Cleopatra for money and military support.

It was a difficult dilemma. Naturally, she hated Caesar's murderers and was inclined to support Dolabella. On the other hand, Cassius was militarily stronger. If he were victorious in neighboring Syria, he might invade Egypt, hoping to seize its treasury to finance the war. And if Cleopatra failed to help him, she could expect no mercy.

In the end, she allowed the four Roman legions that Caesar had stationed in Egypt to leave under their own commander and join Dolabella. She also tried to send him a fleet, but bad weather prevented its sailing. At the same time, she took care not to rebuff Cassius' repeated demands for help—at least not outright. She made excuses, arguing that Egypt was impoverished by famine and plague.

Right after Caesar's death, Mark Antony asked the Senate to forgive the assassins. For this he won praise for most likely averting civil war. Within hours, however, he completely changed his tune.

Scholars have debated for centuries over what he actually said in his funeral oration honoring Caesar, delivered in Rome's marketplace the day after the murder. According to Plutarch, the speech began blandly enough, but *"perceiving the people to be infinitely affected with what he said, he began to mingle with his praises language of commiseration, and horror at what had happened, and, as he was ending his speech, he took the under-clothes of the dead, and held them up, showing them stains of blood and the holes of the many stabs, calling those that had done this act villains and bloody murderers."*

Whatever Antony said, it was enough to send the enraged mob off to burn the houses of the conspirators, causing them to flee Rome forthwith and igniting civil war.

The most famous version of the funeral speech is, of course, the one in Shakespeare's *Julius Caesar*, beginning, "Friends, Romans, countrymen, lend me your ears . . ."

Above: The late 18th-century painting *Death of Caesar* was done by Gaullaume Lethiere of the West Indies islands of Guadeloupe, the son of a freed slave.

Sadly, that was true; the Nile had failed to rise again, and crops had failed.

While she temporized and delayed, the legions that she had sent to Dolabella defected to Cassius. Dolabella was defeated and killed himself.

Egypt was in grave peril. All the surrounding states, Rome's eastern provinces, had declared loyalty to Cassius and Brutus, and now Cassius began making preparations to bring Egypt to heel as well. An invasion was avoided only because, toward the end of 43 B.C., Cassius was summoned by Brutus to an urgent meeting in Asia Minor. The conspirators faced trouble from the West.

When Octavian returned to Rome following the assassination, he had been able to gather a coalition of Caesar's followers (called Caesarians) and republicans, and he drove Antony out of Italy and into Gaul. But in this struggle there was a third principal to contend with: Marcus Aemilius Lepidus, who had been Caesar's master of the horse, or military second in command. Lepidus sided with Antony, bringing with him all of Rome's western provinces. Octavian, at risk of losing everything, decided to make peace and bide his time. In November of 43 B.C., he joined with Antony and Lepidus in the Second Triumvirate, which was to rule jointly with dictatorial powers for five years. Then all three turned their attention to avenging Caesar's death.

The showdown came in the fall of 42 B.C. near the Macedonian town of Philippi. The Caesarians, under Antony, decisively defeated the conspirators and their republican forces. Now Brutus and Cassius were dead, and Antony, Octavian, and Lepidus set about dividing the Roman world among themselves.

Octavian took Rome and the western provinces, Lepidus north

Young Octavian, shown here in a marble sculpture by 19th-century artist Edmonia Lewis, was still in his teens when he learned that his great-uncle, Julius Caesar, had declared him his adopted son and heir. Mark Antony was among the many Romans who at first found it laughable that this sickly boy might actually intend to rule the Roman empire.

Africa, and Antony Rome's eastern client states. The division suited Antony quite well, since, unlike most Romans, he loved the exotic East.

He soon set out to take command of his holdings, establishing himself eventually in the city of Tarsus in Asia Minor. There were many administrative items on his agenda, and one of the more interesting ones had to do with the queen of Egypt. He sent for her, demanding rather harshly that she come to Tarsus and account for her failure to offer Egypt's full backing to the Triumvirate in the latest civil war.

This was not entirely fair. Toward the end of the war, Cleopatra had, in fact, cast her lot with the Caesarians, despite her concern that Octavian was a potential threat to her son. Even with ships sent by Cassius blockading her harbor, she had assembled a large, well-equipped fleet and sailed in command of it herself to join Antony and Octavian in Greece. The fleet ran the blockade successfully, only to fall victim to a storm off the African coast. She was trying to ready another fleet when events at Philippi decided the war's outcome.

She could explain all this to Antony, of course, but she was in no hurry to try: The queen of Egypt was not to be summoned like a common housemaid. She declined to respond to his command; she would let him wait for awhile. When she did go to Tarsus, it would be in her own time and on her own terms.

For the moment, Egypt and its ruler were safe. As to the future, it had become clear that Mark Antony was the Roman whom Cleopatra would have to deal with. She was sure that she could manage that well enough.

Chapter V
THE LAST PHARAOH

It was Mark Antony's misfortune in life to be so readily defined by what he was not: He was not Julius Caesar. Antony was bright (but not brilliant, like Caesar), brave in battle (but not a military genius, like Caesar), and loved by his men (but not worshiped, like Caesar). He had certain advantages of birth and fortune, but (unlike Caesar) he lacked the drive and discipline to make the most of them.

Shortly after Caesar's death, the Senate declared him a god. Antony was no god. He was endearingly, exasperatingly human. Ostentatious, swaggering, generous to a fault, he was capable of a casual cruelty and thoughtlessness that belied his fundamentally kind heart, his trusting and easygoing good nature.

His patrician family claimed divine descent from the demigod Hercules, and in looks and manner, for good and ill, Antony resembled the legendary hero enough to make the kinship seem plausible. He looked a bit like the traditional statuary Hercules—the broad brow, aquiline nose, and full beard—and he loved to affect a Herculean costume, his sword belt slung low on his hips over his tunic to emphasize his magnificent physique. And, like Hercules, Antony was by turns loyal, gentle, strong, loutish, violent, and overfond of wine and women, not excluding his friends' wives from time to time. He was at his best in adversity; lacking a crisis, he tended to be lazy and rudderless.

As a youth Antony fell into bad company, and his drunkenness and generally offensive behavior lost him a good many

Meeting of Antony and Cleopatra is the title of this 1645 painting by France's Sebastien Bourdon. The camels and the obelisk toward the left of the picture—details that would evoke Egypt in the 17th-century European mind—suggest that this particular meeting takes place in Alexandria.

friends in Rome. He went to Greece, there to study military science and rhetoric. (He was fond of the Eastern style of oratory; its florid excess suited his temperament.) Later, Gabinius invited him to join the expedition to restore Auletes to the throne in Egypt, and Antony served with exceptional courage, thus beginning his rise in Roman power circles.

His soldiery so impressed Caesar that after the battle of Pharsalus, he sent Antony to Rome as his second in command. In that post Antony was a failure, however, alienating respectable Romans with his public carousing, his endless hangovers, his consorting with actresses, musicians, and other lowlifes. He fell from favor with Caesar but was later able to ingratiate himself again to such a degree that by the time of the dictator's death, Antony was well situated politically to succeed him. Such an outcome would surely have pleased his third wife, the beautiful Fulvia, a strong-minded and ambitious woman who aimed to cure her husband of his bad habits and mold him into a world leader.

Whatever his flaws, the potential was certainly there. Antony was around forty at the time of Caesar's murder, twice Octavian's age, with far more experience in both governance and war. He was the hero of Philippi, the conqueror of the conspirators. Octavian had been too ill to take part in that battle; in fact, he was so sickly that many people thought he would die young. Antony may have thought so himself. In any event, he discounted Octavian as a boy who owed everything to his name. In this case, as in several others, Antony was a bad judge of character.

He was, however, a good judge of territory. When the triumvirs were dividing up the Roman world,

This Hellenistic bronze statue of Hercules emphasizes the hero's great strength. Along with their powerful bodies, Hercules and Antony had several personality traits in common. Both were said to be impulsive, but genuinely penitent when shown the error of their ways. And both were susceptible to the charms of strong women.
Right: A bust of Mark Antony.

Antony, with first choice, took the East, with all its fabulous wealth. His share included Greece, Asia Minor (the Roman provinces of Asia and Cilicia), Bithynia and Pontus to the north and east, and Syria. Egypt was still nominally independent, but it lay within his sphere of influence.

Along with affording near-endless resources for whatever new military ventures Antony might undertake, the East was also congenial to his luxury-loving nature. His fondness for the Greek way of life was unfeigned, and it was wholly returned: The Hellenistic world welcomed its new governor with open arms.

Antony spent the winter of 42–41 B.C. in Greece, then traveled across the Aegean to Ephesus, there to be hailed joyfully as the New Dionysus, the bringer of peace and plenty. (No doubt he relished being conceived of as a god, especially since Octavian, as the adopted son of the deified Caesar, was styling himself as the son of a god.) The worshipful greeting was repeated many times over as Antony continued his eastern progress, cementing his position as the most influential man in the world, first among the triumvirs. The future looked bright, and doubtless he believed he would eclipse Octavian and Lepidus permanently with the successful execution of his next feat: He planned to take up Caesar's aborted quest to conquer the powerful Parthian empire.

For this massive enterprise, however, he needed Egypt's backing, and it was to gain it—as well as to complain about her rather tepid support of the Caesarians against the conspirators—that he sent for Cleopatra.

William Shakespeare, relying on an account from Plutarch, wrote some of his most sublime poetry in recounting Cleopatra's entry into Tarsus in his *Antony and Cleopatra:*

The barge she sat in, like a burnish'd throne, • Burn'd on the water. The poop was beaten gold; • Purpled the sails, and so perfumed that • The winds were love-sick with them. The oars were silver, • Which to the tune of flutes kept stroke, and made • The water which they beat to follow faster, • As amorous of their strokes. • For her own person, • It beggar'd all description; she did lie • In her pavilion—cloth-of-gold, of tissue, • O'er-picturing that Venus where we see • The fancy outwork nature.

Above: **This port scene of Cleopatra setting out for Tarsus was painted by 17th-century artist Claude Lorraine.**

The Cleopatra laying plans in her royal palace to meet with Antony was quite different from the inexperienced young exile laying plans in her desert tent to conquer Caesar seven years earlier. She was now twenty-eight, a mother, a woman who had known love and survived the loss of it, a queen secure in her power and confident of her personal allure. She had gone to Caesar as a fugitive. She would go to Antony as a goddess.

After ignoring several impatient summons, she finally agreed to a meeting at the ancient city of Tarsus in Cilicia. Under her direction a huge royal ship was prepared—painted gold, rigged with sails tinged purple by the precious dyes of Tyre, propelled by silver oars. On this floating palace she made her way across the Mediterranean and into a lagoon of the river Cydnus.

The river banks were soon teeming with people gaping at the spectacle. While beautiful serving women dressed in the fluttering tunics of nymphs attended to steering Cleopatra's ship, the silver oars dipped in rhythm to the music of pipes and lutes. Each breath of wind sent the rich fragrance of incense wafting toward the shore. On deck a canopy of woven gold had been erected, and beneath it, dressed as Aphrodite, Cleopatra reclined on a couch, fanned languidly on either side by handsome boys costumed as cupids.

Antony, awaiting the queen in Tarsus' marketplace, found himself virtually alone, deserted as the populace scurried toward the river in response to cries that Aphrodite had come to revel with Dionysus. When she didn't appear, he sent word inviting her to dine with him that evening; she politely replied that she'd prefer that he and his friends come to her on the ship.

That night, Antony and his entourage arrived to find a dozen tables laid in the ship's dining hall, all set with golden, bejeweled plates and chalices. Tapestries woven of gold and silver thread hung here and there, and—most spectacular of all—tiny torches had been suspended from the rigging to form fanciful designs that glittered on all sides. Antony was dazzled, as he was meant to be, and awed all the

Neither Cleopatra nor Antony seems to be particularly enjoying dinner in this 18th-century rendering of one of their banquets, *Following spread.* Perhaps the problem is the stiffly formal setting or the heavy European clothing imagined by the artist, Giovanni Battista Tiepolo.

more when Cleopatra casually informed him that the luxuries laid before him were his to keep.

He entertained her ashore the following night, though in considerably less sumptuous style, and she received him again on the ship on the third night and on the fourth, when he and his men found themselves treading a deck carpeted more than a foot deep in roses. Each night she made him a gift of the precious dinnerware, and she distributed among the other guests presents only slightly less opulent.

Cleopatra probably viewed this outflow of Egyptian capital as a shrewd investment, for it was intended to impress not only Antony but all the East, hinting at a sort of sacred alliance between Egypt and Rome. In the Hellenistic mind, Dionysus was equated with Osiris and Aphrodite with Isis. Thus in visiting the New Dionysus in the guise of the Greek goddess of love, the queen was enhancing her status internationally by implying a marital connection on the divine plane. All the Levant would have understood it as such and would have viewed the lavish hospitality as suitably celebratory of such a union.

Moreover, Cleopatra was cleverly appealing to every notable aspect of Antony's nature: his vanity, his love of drama and display, his susceptibility to luxury—and to women. History does not record exactly when the queen and the triumvir became lovers in Tarsus, but it hardly matters. The consummation was a foregone conclusion.

Affairs of state seemed to recede from Antony's mind at this point, but not necessarily from Cleopatra's. However pleasant the interlude in Tarsus, she was also there to do business. For her help in the upcoming war against the Parthians, she had a price. She explained to Antony that while she hadn't helped the conspirators in the recent war, she had reason to believe that her sister Arsinoë was guilty of that very thing: She had persuaded Serapion, the governor of Cyprus, to aid Brutus and Cassius. Arsinoë was summarily dragged from her sanctuary at Ephesus by Antony's men and executed. Serapion was killed, too. So was Arsinoë's other pawn,

The Cleopatra laying plans in her royal palace to meet with Antony was quite different from the inexperienced young exile laying plans in her desert tent to conquer Caesar seven years earlier. She was now twenty-eight, a mother, a woman who had known love and survived the loss of it, a queen secure in her power and confident of her personal allure. She had gone to Caesar as a fugitive. She would go to Antony as a goddess.

After ignoring several impatient summons, she finally agreed to a meeting at the ancient city of Tarsus in Cilicia. Under her direction a huge royal ship was prepared—painted gold, rigged with sails tinged purple by the precious dyes of Tyre, propelled by silver oars. On this floating palace she made her way across the Mediterranean and into a lagoon of the river Cydnus.

The river banks were soon teeming with people gaping at the spectacle. While beautiful serving women dressed in the fluttering tunics of nymphs attended to steering Cleopatra's ship, the silver oars dipped in rhythm to the music of pipes and lutes. Each breath of wind sent the rich fragrance of incense wafting toward the shore. On deck a canopy of woven gold had been erected, and beneath it, dressed as Aphrodite, Cleopatra reclined on a couch, fanned languidly on either side by handsome boys costumed as cupids.

Antony, awaiting the queen in Tarsus' marketplace, found himself virtually alone, deserted as the populace scurried toward the river in response to cries that Aphrodite had come to revel with Dionysus. When she didn't appear, he sent word inviting her to dine with him that evening; she politely replied that she'd prefer that he and his friends come to her on the ship.

That night, Antony and his entourage arrived to find a dozen tables laid in the ship's dining hall, all set with golden, bejeweled plates and chalices. Tapestries woven of gold and silver thread hung here and there, and—most spectacular of all—tiny torches had been suspended from the rigging to form fanciful designs that glittered on all sides. Antony was dazzled, as he was meant to be, and awed all the

Neither Cleopatra nor Antony seems to be particularly enjoying dinner in this 18th-century rendering of one of their banquets, *Following spread.* Perhaps the problem is the stiffly formal setting or the heavy European clothing imagined by the artist, Giovanni Battista Tiepolo.

more when Cleopatra casually informed him that the luxuries laid before him were his to keep.

He entertained her ashore the following night, though in considerably less sumptuous style, and she received him again on the ship on the third night and on the fourth, when he and his men found themselves treading a deck carpeted more than a foot deep in roses. Each night she made him a gift of the precious dinnerware, and she distributed among the other guests presents only slightly less opulent.

Cleopatra probably viewed this outflow of Egyptian capital as a shrewd investment, for it was intended to impress not only Antony but all the East, hinting at a sort of sacred alliance between Egypt and Rome. In the Hellenistic mind, Dionysus was equated with Osiris and Aphrodite with Isis. Thus in visiting the New Dionysus in the guise of the Greek goddess of love, the queen was enhancing her status internationally by implying a marital connection on the divine plane. All the Levant would have understood it as such and would have viewed the lavish hospitality as suitably celebratory of such a union.

Moreover, Cleopatra was cleverly appealing to every notable aspect of Antony's nature: his vanity, his love of drama and display, his susceptibility to luxury—and to women. History does not record exactly when the queen and the triumvir became lovers in Tarsus, but it hardly matters. The consummation was a foregone conclusion.

Affairs of state seemed to recede from Antony's mind at this point, but not necessarily from Cleopatra's. However pleasant the interlude in Tarsus, she was also there to do business. For her help in the upcoming war against the Parthians, she had a price. She explained to Antony that while she hadn't helped the conspirators in the recent war, she had reason to believe that her sister Arsinoë was guilty of that very thing: She had persuaded Serapion, the governor of Cyprus, to aid Brutus and Cassius. Arsinoë was summarily dragged from her sanctuary at Ephesus by Antony's men and executed. Serapion was killed, too. So was Arsinoë's other pawn,

the pseudo-Ptolemy XIII. With her sister dead, Cleopatra was, at last, the only survivor of Auletes' six children.

The queen returned to Alexandria, and after a brief trip to Syria, Antony followed her. He planned to spend the winter of 41 B.C. in Egypt. As it turned out, he stayed a year.

For Cleopatra it was a magical time, a kind of belated girlhood of carefree, unrestricted play— absent in the hazardous days of her youth. She devised a never-ending round of entertainments for her lover: days of public games and hunting and fishing, nights of feasting and gambling. Sometimes the two would dress as commoners and roam the streets of Alexandria or visit the taverns of nearby Canopus, the resort town at the mouth of the Nile. With companions drawn from Alexandria's intelligentsia and social elite, they formed a society that they called the Inimitable Livers, dedicated to the enjoyment of life's richness. And if, by chance, Antony found that all such pleasures palled, there remained Cleopatra herself. For these two handsome, vital people in their prime, the sexual bond must have been very strong.

Even so, Antony couldn't stay. While he had been idling in Alexandria, the Parthians had overrun the Roman provinces of Syria

Greek geographer Strabo described Alexandria's Great Harbor, *below*: *"At the entrance, on the right hand, are the island and the tower Pharos, and on the other hand are the reefs and also the promontory Lochias, with a royal palace upon it, and on sailing into the harbour one comes, on the left, to the inner royal palaces, which are continuous with those on Lochias and have groves and numerous lodges painted in various colours."*

and Judea and made inroads into Asia Minor. He traveled to Asia Minor, where he heard even worse news. Without his knowledge, his head-strong wife and his brother in Italy had provoked an uprising against Octavian. They had been soundly defeated, and Fulvia fled to Greece. It was to Athens, therefore, that the furious Antony headed in the spring of 40 B.C., to learn the details of Fulvia's machinations. After a stormy meeting with her, he set out for Italy to try to heal the breach with Octavian. He would never see his wife again; she fell ill and died a few months later.

However unfortunate for Anthony, these developments were welcome news to Cleopatra. She'd aimed all along to make him break with Octavian, whom she always saw as Caesarion's rival to ultimately succeed Caesar. Her revived dream of a world-shaping alliance between Rome and Egypt now depended on Antony: He must get rid of Octavian and throw his full support behind her son. Fulvia's death thus seemed wonderfully opportune, freeing Antony to marry her. Whether Rome recognized the union or not, it would draw him closer to her and drive a deeper wedge between him and Octavian.

PLUTARCH'S CAST OF CHARACTERS

The Greek historian Plutarch (A.D. 46–120) was a philosopher and biographer who, though well traveled, chose to spend his life in the small town of his birth, Chaironeia. He served many years as a priest at Delphi and, though Rome conferred high honors for his writings, he always maintained a strong Greek identity.

His most famous work, entitled *Parallel Lives of the Noble Greeks and Romans,* better known as *Lives,* was a collection of forty-four paired biographies. Focusing on morality, Plutarch crafted comparisons of Greek and Roman leaders that connected success and failure with the individuals' strength or weakness of character.

An ancient catalog of Plutarch's works lists about one hundred more pieces than survive today. While his writings remain the best surviving source for the historical events he wrote about, his focus on character rather than structural forces has provided fodder for centuries of writers and artists.

***Above:* Detail from *The Disembarkation of Cleopatra at Tarsus* by Dutch painter Gerard de Lairesse.**

Bernard Camier cradles a wine amphora found at the site of an ancient shipwreck. It features a narrow neck and two handles rising close to the mouth of the vessel—two characteristics that typify amphorae. This particular artifact originated in Crete and dates back to between the 1st century B.C. and 1st century A.D. Clay containers such as these were commonly used throughout the Mediterranean region during ancient times to store and transport foodstuffs, including olive oil, wine, salt-fish, and fish sauce (garum). Whether long and cylindrical or tear-drop shaped, their bodies were designed to facilitate handling and stowage aboard ships. Amphorae handles or stoppers often featured stamps that identified shipper, recipient, or contents.

HEROD THE GREAT

The Herod who figures in Cleopatra's story is best known in the West as the biblical tyrant who, late in his reign, tried to eliminate the newborn Jesus by ordering the slaughter of all the male infants in Judea. He was, however, a much more complex personality than that single story indicates.

Although he ruled a nation of Jews, Herod himself was an Idumaean Arab; his father and grandfather had been governors of the province of Idumaea in southern Judea, where the people had been forced to convert to Judaism in the century before Herod's birth. Like the Ptolemies, Herod's family had forged ties with Rome and viewed themselves as part of a wider, Hellenistic world beyond Judea.

Herod was serving as viceroy to the Judean ruler in 40 B.C.—placed in that office by his friend Mark Antony—when the Parthians overran his country. He fled for his life to Egypt, and there for the first time met Cleopatra. She helped him get to Rome, where he hoped to rally support to reclaim his country. He was thirty-two at the time— handsome, charming, and brilliant— and he became a great favorite in Rome's aristocratic circles. With Antony's backing, the Roman Senate declared him king of Judea—and then left him on his own to make the title mean something.

He did. An able general, he ousted the Parthians, then killed off the enfeebled remnants of the Hasmonean dynasty that had previously ruled Judea. He expanded his territory to include Samaria, Galilee, and much of Syria. He began obsessively building, concentrating first on Jerusalem. Working around the inner sanctum that was all that remained of the old temple of Solomon, he constructed a vast new temple whose beauty was a source of awe throughout the Mediterranean world. (Its west wall, the so-called Wailing Wall, still stands.) He built himself a palace in Jerusalem, a summer palace in Jericho, and a line of fortress palaces in the desert, including one at Masada. After Antony's defeat at Actium, Herod switched his allegiance to Octavian, and in his honor designed and built the port city of Caesarea, complete with a man-made harbor.

Nominally a Jew, Herod was nevertheless a Hellenistic monarch to the core—sophisticated, luxury-loving, crafty—and as murderous as any Ptolemy. He killed one of his ten wives and three of his sixteen sons for suspected treachery (causing his patron, now called Caesar Augustus, to remark that it was "better to be Herod's pig than Herod's son"), and he brutally suppressed dissent among fundamentalist Jews who hated him as an outsider, a blasphemer, a tyrant, and a Roman puppet who was corrupting Jewish life.

As he aged, Herod became ever more paranoid and bloodthirsty, and toward the end of his life, in constant pain from a cancerous ailment that was eating him alive, he went quite mad.

As he lay dying in Jericho in A.D. 4, he commanded that the heads of all Judea's leading families be rounded up and held hostage, to be murdered upon his death: If Judea would not weep for him, he said, it would weep nevertheless. The order was never carried out.

Left: James Jacques Joseph Tissot's painting of the *Temple of Herod in Our Lord's Time*, circa 1886–96.

In her singlemindedness, it may never have occurred to Cleopatra that perhaps she'd chosen the wrong triumvir. She and Octavian had much in common: their acute intelligence, their tenacity, their relentless thirst for power. And if others underestimated the young Roman, the queen most likely did not. She'd known Caesar well enough to understand that he must have seen something extraordinary in his nephew to leave Rome in his hands. But it was too late for second thoughts. Cleopatra had fallen in love with Antony and was pregnant by him. A few months after his departure, she gave birth to twins, a boy and a girl whom she named Alexander Helios (the Sun) and Cleopatra Selene (the Moon). Now she could only wait, trusting that the spell she had cast on Antony would be strong enough to bring him back to her and to their children.

For news of Antony's activities in Rome, Cleopatra relied on an Egyptian astrologer whom she had inserted into his ranks. When the spy's report came back to her, it was shattering. There had been much bickering among the triumvirs, but in the end they reaffirmed their pact. This was bad enough, but the item that followed it was devastating: To seal the alliance, Antony had married Octavian's sister.

Cleopatra must have reacted initially more as a woman than a queen—with rage, pain, and ravening jealousy. Octavia, the new bride, was younger than she, beautiful and highly intelligent, and respected far and wide for her irreproachable virtue. If the queen had any faint hope that the marriage was merely one of convenience, it vanished within the year with the news that Octavia was pregnant. She and her husband were living in Athens, where Antony was once again enjoying his round of games and entertainments while his armies won a couple of preliminary victories against the Parthians.

But whatever shame and anger Cleopatra may have suffered because of his betrayal, her native pragmatism eventually took hold. The time would come, she knew, when he would need Egypt again. And that meant he would need her.

⊠

Their separation lasted three years. During that time, the alliance between Antony and Octavian grew increasingly strained; yet it held, largely due to Octavia's calming influence on both her husband and her brother. At the Italian city of Tarentum in the summer of 37 B.C., the Triumvirate was renewed for another five years. That fall, however, Antony left Octavia—then pregnant with their second child—and sailed for Antioch in Syria. There, he once again sent for Cleopatra.

She decided to go to him, just as she had gone to Tarsus four years before. But this time she would drive a much harder bargain: If he wanted her—and the financial and military aid that only she could provide—he would have to cede to Egypt almost all the lands held by the Ptolemies at the height of their power two centuries before.

So Cleopatra, with her children, sailed to meet Antony, and at Antioch their passion reignited. They enjoyed a year together in the lovely old city—not as lovers, this time, but as man and wife. Cleopatra had learned from her liaison with Caesar, and from Antony's abandonment, how little security was to be had from love alone. This time she demanded marriage. Antony acceded, and the two were wed according to an Eastern rite that permitted polygamy.

Predictably, the marriage scandalized Rome. Much sympathy was lavished on Octavia, who bore her humiliation in graceful silence. Cleopatra drew only vituperation; she was decried as a wanton sorceress who had now unmanned a second noble Roman. Octavian was particularly outraged—publicly, at least. In private, he may well have welcomed this development as a propaganda coup. Public disgust with Antony would be useful when the Triumvirate at last disintegrated, as Octavian surely knew it must: Like Cleopatra, he understood that, in the end, only one man could rule in Rome.

For the moment, however, Cleopatra was not particularly concerned with Rome's opinion, or Octavian's. She had Antony, and through him she had managed to regain for Egypt most of the ancestral lands of the Ptolemies. Among her new holdings were several wealthy coastal cities in Syria and Phoenicia, the state of Ituraea, parts of coastal Cilicia, several cities bordering Judea, and the greater part of the Judean coastline. She had also acquired valuable farmland near Jericho, a source of exportable dates and of balsam trees that yielded an expensive balm, the biblical balm of Gilead.

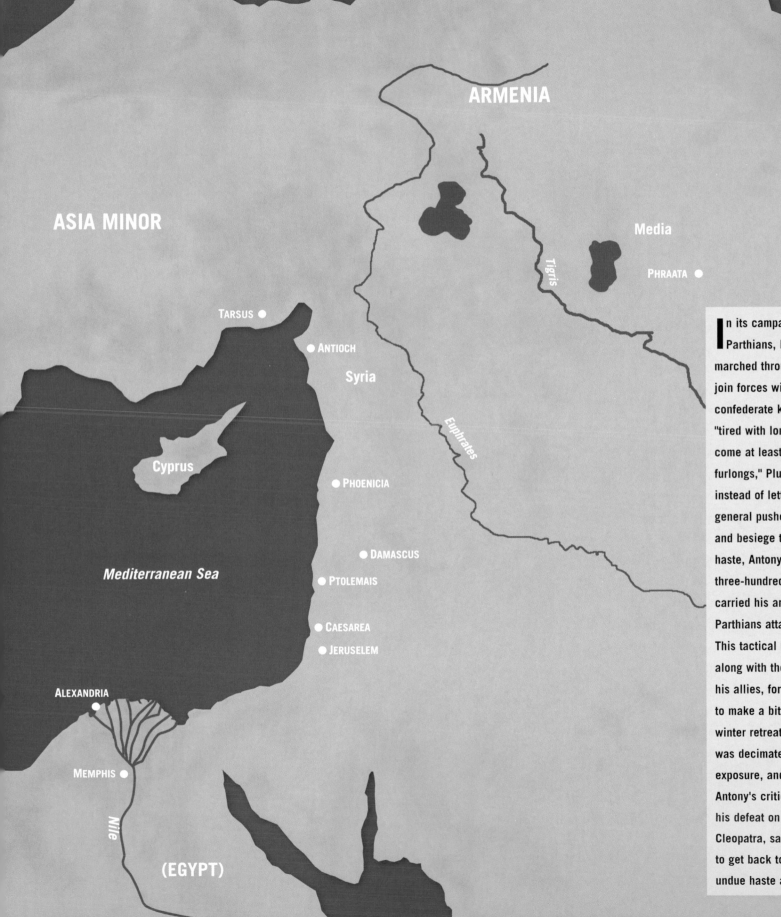

Caspian Sea

ARMENIA

PARTHIA

ASIA MINOR

Media

Tigris

PHRAATA ●

TARSUS ●

● ANTIOCH

Syria

Euphrates

Cyprus

● PHOENICIA

Mediterranean Sea

● DAMASCUS

● PTOLEMAIS

● CAESAREA

● JERUSELEM

ALEXANDRIA
●

Nile

MEMPHIS ●

(EGYPT)

In its campaign against the Parthians, Mark Antony's army marched through Arabia to Armenia to join forces with the troops of several confederate kings. Antony's men were "tired with long marches, having come at least eight thousand furlongs," Plutarch reported, but instead of letting them rest, their general pushed on to invade Media and besiege the city of Phraata. In his haste, Antony left behind a vital three-hundred-wagon train that carried his army's siege engines. The Parthians attacked and destroyed it. This tactical blunder and others, along with the treachery of some of his allies, forced Antony and his men to make a bitter twenty-seven-day winter retreat, during which the army was decimated by disease, hunger, exposure, and Parthian arrows. Antony's critics were quick to blame his defeat on his infatuation with Cleopatra, saying that his eagerness to get back to her explained his undue haste and bad judgment.

She wanted Judea in its entirety, since it had once belonged to her dynasty, but Antony withstood her persistent efforts to get it. He'd gone to great pains to install on the throne at Jerusalem a very effective young king, his friend and ally Herod, and he planned to keep him there. Rome was beginning to fear Cleopatra's power, and at this point even Antony seemed to feel a need to keep it in check: A strong Judea would counterbalance Egypt's primacy in the Levant.

There was also a certain logic in Antony's choice of the territories he did cede to his wife. Much of the land was rich in timber, and timber is necessary for building ships. Antony had resumed his preparations to attack the Parthians, and Cleopatra was to build him a fleet.

Antony set out from Syria in the spring of 36 B.C. for the Parthian campaign. He intended it to be the greatest of all imperial wars, his chance to prove himself Caesar's military equal and worthy successor. With an elaborate royal retinue, Cleopatra went with him as far as the Euphrates, returning to Alexandria by way of Judea to inspect her new holdings there. By some accounts, Herod took this opportunity to try to assassinate her and, failing, politely escorted her to the Egyptian border. Such behavior would have been typical of the thirty-two-year-old monarch, who was both murderous and diplomatically deft.

Back in Egypt, Cleopatra bore Antony another son, Ptolemy Philadelphus, and awaited word from the east of a magnificent victory that would secure the futures of all her children. But the Parthian war proved a catastrophe. In a tactical blunder, Antony divided his forces, leaving part of his army prey to the treachery of his supposed ally, the Armenian king Artavasdes, whose troops turned on the Romans and slaughtered them. Many more legionaries died under the arrows of the famed Parthian archers or perished of disease or exposure during a bitter, month-long winter retreat to Syria. In all, Antony lost forty thousand cavalry and twenty thousand infantry.

From Syria, he sent for Cleopatra to bring money and provisions for his men. She complied, but she must have had grave misgivings about Antony's future, and her own. His chief claim to superiority over Octavian was his supposed military prowess. Now, in the greatest wartime test of his life, he had failed dismally. True, Octavian wasn't much of a warrior, but he commanded a man who was. Marcus Vipsanius Agrippa, his friend since boyhood, had evolved into an admiral of prodigious talent. While Antony was being crushed by the Parthians, Agrippa seized the Sicilian stronghold of Pompey the Great's last surviving son, the rebellious Sextus, whose own fleet had beaten back all previous assaults.

As Agrippa waged war, Octavian maneuvered on the political front, forcing Lepidus into retirement and taking control of north Africa. Only two triumvirs remained, and Octavian, supreme in the West, seemed to have the upper hand.

If Octavian lacked promise as a general, he was nevertheless one of the most brilliant politicians and propagandists the world had ever known. He began demonstrating this when Antony sent dispatches to Rome trying to put the Parthian disaster in a favorable (and utterly fictitious) light. Octavian knew quite well how thorough his colleague's defeat had been, but he never questioned

DECEITFUL LIAISON

Antony never wanted war with Octavian, and he persisted in forgiving his fellow triumvir, no matter how many times Octavian betrayed him or broke his word to him, until forgiveness was no longer an option. Antony had "much simplicity in his character," Plutarch notes, and was "prone to trust frankly in all about him." Even the warnings of Cleopatra—who trusted almost no one, and least of all Octavian—could not hurry her lover toward the inevitable showdown with Octavian for control of Rome.

Above: **Antony himself would doubtless have relished the idyllic scene in this Brussels tapestry by Karel Van Mander, showing a bearded Mark Antony and a young Octavian wearing laurel wreaths, their hands clasped in friendship.**

Left: **A statue of Octavian.**

Antony's lies. Rather, he insisted that Rome offer official thanks to its conquering hero. The ploy was useful in two ways. First, it made Octavian appear gracious. Second, and more pertinently, it allowed him to suggest that Antony could now recruit men and settle his veterans in his vast new territories—not in Italy, Octavian's own power base. The shrewd move damaged Antony militarily, but he could hardly complain about it without revealing his own duplicity.

Octavian next arranged that the Senate confer on both him and Antony the honor of holding banquets in the Temple of Concord, which they would attend with their wives and children. He knew, of course, that Antony wouldn't come, and his absence would call attention to his continuing liaison with Cleopatra.

Lest anyone in Rome miss the point, Octavian engineered yet another coup. He dispatched Octavia from Italy to Syria with provisions for Antony's decimated army, along with ships and two thousand soldiers. In Rome, the gesture looked generous. In fact, however, Octavian had promised his brother-in-law twenty thousand legionaries, and the contingent he sent was a blatant insult. Octavia got as far as Athens before receiving a letter from her husband telling her that she should send the supplies to Syria but that she herself should go back to Rome. Most Romans concluded, as Octavian meant them to, that Antony was once again spurning his true wife in favor of his Egyptian whore. Meanwhile, Octavia herself inadvertently made matters worse for Antony with her own impeccable behavior. She dutifully continued to keep his house in Rome and to care for his children, both hers and Fulvia's. The populace grumbled ever-louder about her husband's abominable treatment of such a good woman.

Antony and Cleopatra returned to Alexandria, and in 34 B.C. he eased some of the sting of the Parthian defeat by successfully invading Armenia, capturing the treacherous King Artavasdes and his family, and looting his palace. In the fall, Cleopatra welcomed her husband home with an elaborate triumph. There was the usual public feasting and the triumphal parade, in which Antony, dressed as Dionysus, drew his war chariot up before the golden throne where Cleopatra sat, attired as Isis. Alexandria was delighted with the spectacle. Rome was not: For a Roman general to hold a triumph in any city other than Rome was scandalous.

This outrage, however, was but a pale prelude to the one that followed. A few days after the triumph, another ceremony was staged, this one in Alexandria's huge stadium, the Gymnasium. Within it stood a two-level silver platform bearing six golden thrones. On the top tier sat Antony and Cleopatra, and on the level beneath them were the children: Caesarion, now thirteen, the six-year-old twins, and little Ptolemy Philadelphus, two. The children were dressed in various native costumes of the East; their role in the ceremony was to officially receive from Antony the thrones of the lands he had already ceded to Cleopatra, along with Cyprus, the newly conquered Armenia, and the yet-to-be-conquered Parthia. Cleopatra would act as regent for all of them. He also announced new titles: Cleopatra would henceforth be Queen of Kings and Caesarion King of Kings. Most important of all, perhaps, Antony stated that Caesarion was the son—the legitimate son—of Julius Caesar. In so doing, he offered a direct insult to Octavian, suggesting that Caesarion was Caesar's true heir and Octavian a usurper.

The ceremony became known as the Donations of Alexandria, and in Rome it provided fresh and abundant fodder for Octavian's propaganda mill. Antony had given away huge stretches of Roman territory to his grasping Oriental mistress and her bastards. Could there be any doubt that she meant to rule Rome as well? Could there be any doubt that the wiles that had once ensnared Caesar had now brought the noble Antony to debauchery and ruin? Was he not now more Egyptian than Roman?

Antony, long absent from Rome, still had defenders among the people and in the Senate, but their numbers were dwindling, and attacks on them by Octavian's partisans grew more and more acrimonious. Once again, Rome stood on the brink of civil war.

In 33 B.C., Antony and Cleopatra went to Ephesus to begin preparing for the coming conflict. Antony's forces were formidable: seventy-five thousand legionaries, twenty-five thousand auxiliary light infantry, and twelve thousand cavalry. In addition, he had a fleet of five hundred warships and three hundred merchant vessels. Some two hundred of the fighting ships were Egyptian, and Cleopatra had her own flagship and a personal squadron of sixty other vessels. The daunting assemblage of military resources probably enhanced Antony's support in Rome, where some were convinced that he might still emerge victorious from a showdown with Octavian. Almost four hundred senators went to join him in Ephesus. In the summer of 32 B.C., however, Antony committed another strategic blunder: To make his rift with Octavian complete, he divorced Octavia. Cleopatra was no doubt pleased, but the Antonian senators were aghast. Most of them returned to Rome and to Octavian.

Unfortunately, two of the defectors had acted as witnesses when Antony drew up his will. When they told Octavian of its contents, he committed the sacrilege of seizing it by force from the Vestal Virgins, in whose care such documents customarily resided. Octavian then read its contents—or what he said were its contents—to the Senate. Most offensive to that body was Antony's request that if he died in Rome, his corpse should be taken to Alexandria for burial with Cleopatra.

Not long after the reading of the will, with the shock of it still resounding throughout the city, Octavian, dressed in the old-fashioned garb of an earlier Rome, strode to the Field of Mars. There he threw a javelin smeared with blood from the temple of the war god-

dess Bellona. The gesture was the nation's ancient declaration of war against a foreign enemy: Rome's crusade would not be against Antony but against Egypt, against the foreign queen who had bewitched him.

As he gathered his allies from Sicily and Sardinia, Africa and Gaul, Octavian presented himself as the savior of freedom, the guardian of the republic against the monarchists of the East. In fact, as he well knew, the republic was long past reviving. What remained to be decided was which brand of monarchy would prevail: his, or Antony's and Cleopatra's.

They, meanwhile, were finishing their preparations in Ephesus. Those had gone fairly smoothly, but not without a certain amount of bickering. Several of Antony's advisors wanted him to send the queen back to Egypt, arguing that a woman had no business taking part in the planning and execution of war. But Cleopatra had no intention of leaving. She was, after all, financing this venture, and she meant to keep an eye on her investment. As was generally the case, she got her way.

Their work in Ephesus done, she and Antony journeyed to the island of Samos and then to Athens for a round of celebrations and festivities. It wasn't a matter of dancing in the shadow of the sword; the pair fully expected that the war would end with their ruling the Roman world. Rather, the festivals had religious overtones, and participating in them was the ancient way in which Hellenistic rulers readied themselves for war.

MACEDONIA

Mt. Olympus ^

ONCHESMUS

BUTHROTUM

Corcyra
(Corsica)

PHOTICE

Ionian Islands

EPIRUS

METROPOLIS

ACTIUM

Leucas

STRATUS

AMPHISSA

OENIADE

NAUPACTUS

DELPHI

CIRRHA

Cephalenia

AEGEAN SEA

ACHAEA

Ionian Sea

ELEUSIS

MARATHON

PATRAE

Gulf of
Corinthus

PIRAEUS

CORINTHUS
(Corinth)

Zacynthus

ATHENAE
(ATHENS)

Andros

Aegina

Mt. Laurium

Tinos

OLYMPIA

ARGOS

Peloponnesus
(Greece)

N

CYCLADES

MEGALOPOLIS

LEGEND

Ancient name
(Modern name)

MESSENE

Naxe

SPARTA

Paros

METHONE

Siphnos

LAS

0   120km

0   75mi

Melos

ASOPUS

Thera

BATTLE OF ACTIUM

GOMAROS
BAY

OCTAVIAN'S CAMP

IONIAN
SEA

Nicopolis

GULF OF AMBRACIA

Octavian's
blockading
fleet

Pantokrator
Fort
^

ACTIUM PENINSULA

^ Fort

Antony's
anchorage

ANTONY'S CAMP

Cleopatra's
fleet

In the fall of 32 B.C., Antony and Cleopatra set up a winter camp at the town of Patrae on the Gulf of Corinth. Patrae was a link in a chain of coastal and island naval outposts that had been established by Antony and stretched from Corcyra on Greece's Ionian coast southward almost to north Africa. The chain would be a supply route for goods coming from Egypt and also would serve as a defensive line against Octavian's ships. The bulk of the Antonian army moved northwestward to another link in the chain, the coastal town of Actium in Epirus. Actium stood on the southern shore of a narrow strait that formed the mouth of the expansive Gulf of Ambracia—perfect harborage, it seemed, for the enormous Egyptian fleet.

In Patrae, Antony confidently awaited Octavian's arrival. His army and navy were larger than Octavian's, and they were well trained and well equipped. If invaders from the west managed to get past his chain of naval fortresses, he could easily conquer them at Actium, either by land or by sea.

In his calculations, however, he failed to factor in Agrippa. In a fast, daring foray, Octavian's brilliant admiral captured the important naval fortress at Methone on the southwest tip of Greece, breaking Antony's defensive chain and disrupting his supply route. From there, Agrippa harried the other stations, drawing off Antony's warships to defend them and allowing Octavian to move his army onshore north of Actium. When Cleopatra and Antony arrived to set up their Actium headquarters, they found Octavian's army encamped half a mile away, on the northern side of the entrance to the Gulf of Ambracia. Agrippa, meanwhile, needed only a few ships to blockade

This bronze prow ornament, called a *rostrum*, from a ship sunk at Actium, was not merely decorative. In battle, such devices were used for ramming other ships.
***Following spread:* A 17th-century depiction of the Battle of Actium by Lorenzo Castro.**

the gulf's constricted entrance and keep Antony's fleet bottled up inside.

Actium, the perfect haven, had turned into the perfect trap.

Antony tried to seize the initiative by crossing the strait and offering battle, but Octavian cleverly refused to fight. There was no need. His supply line to Rome was intact. Antony's to Egypt was broken. Time was on his side.

In the pest-infested heat of the Grecian summer, the situation in the Antonian camp went from bad to worse as the weeks stretched on. Food was scarce, and hundreds of men were ill with malaria or dysentery. Morale was terrible—and defections inevitable. They began as a trickle and soon became a steady stream, as various client princes, and even some of Antony's most trusted generals, went over to Octavian. At the end of August, Antony called a council of war. He must break out of the trap, but would this best be attempted on land or by sea?

His principal general, Canidius Crassus, wanted Antony to march north and try to tempt Octavian into a major land battle in Macedonia or Thrace. Antony was, after all, a land general, and he had no admiral to rival Agrippa. But this meant that Cleopatra would either have to go with him, abandoning her fleet, or stay behind and try to break out by sea with her squadron and the rest of her ships.

The land option was unacceptable to her. It meant separation from Antony, and that she would not endure—because she loved him, perhaps, but also because she may have doubted by now that he could win a pitched battle on land. The Parthian disaster had taught her (if indeed she hadn't known it already) that Antony was, in fact, no Caesar. If he lost, all that she had gained for Egypt—and all she still aspired to—would vanish. If they could break out by sea, at least there was a chance to regroup and fight another day.

She won her point; Actium would be a sea battle. But both Cleopatra and Antony must have known that the best they could expect from it was escape, not victory.

⁂

Due to disease and desertions, Antony lacked enough rowers for the entire fleet. The ships he couldn't man, he burned. After that was done, there remained only 230 vessels of the original 800-ship armada. On September 2, 31 B.C., these began rowing in single file toward the mouth of the Gulf of Ambracia. Antony's ships led the way, and Cleopatra's squadron followed. She herself was on her flagship, the *Antonias,* which also bore the Egyptian war chest of gold, silver, and jewels. All the ships carried sail, a clear indication that their main objective was flight: Ordinarily, warships relied on their rowers; the weight and bulk of sails inhibited maneuverability.

In the Ionian Sea, Octavian's fleet of four hundred ships, commanded by him and Agrippa, lay in wait. At last, the two sides clashed.

As Octavian's ships locked with Antony's, Cleopatra's squadron slipped through the battle and into the open sea. Under full sail, she sped south for Egypt. Antony followed, leaving his own flagship under heavy attack and boarding another ship that rendezvoused with Cleopatra's.

Behind him the two navies continued to grapple for hours, but the outcome was victory for Octavian and Agrippa. Some thirty or forty Antonian ships were sunk, and the rest surrendered.

In the hands of Octavian's propagandists, Actium became an instant legend. According to their version, a cowardly Cleopatra,

A bronze Roman coin minted sometime between 10 B.C. and A.D. 10 shows the profiles of Caesar Augustus—the former Octavian—and his great admiral, Agrippa, *below.* Octavian's lifelong friend, Agrippa was the primary military force behind the young triumvir's rise to power. Later in their lives, Agrippa married Octavian's only child, Julia. They had five children.
Right: Cleopatra meets with Octavian in this 18th-century painting by Louis Gauffier. According to some accounts, the queen tried to seduce her conqueror in a last-ditch effort to save her kingdom for her children.

believing the battle lost, fled to save her own life. And Antony, the love-besotted weakling, dishonored everything sacred to a Roman general by deserting his men in battle to follow her.

It was a wonderfully romantic account, if not exactly a true one. The plan all along had evidently been for Cleopatra and Antony to escape, saving as much of the fleet as they could. When Antony made good his getaway, his ships were supposed to disengage and follow. As it turned out, the opposing fleet's numerical superiority made this impossible.

Flattering Octavian, the propagandists also portrayed Actium as a climactic and decisive clash of titans, in which the brave and virtuous West put to rout the degraded East. In fact, the cause of Cleopatra and Antony had been all but lost months before with Methone's fall to Agrippa. Actium had merely been the partly successful running of a blockade.

Cleopatra seemed to see it that way, but Antony was deeply depressed. He had, he knew, dishonored himself by leaving men under his command to die. And there was no good news to lift his spirits as the diminished fleet neared north Africa. Messengers rowed out to report that his land army in Greece had surrendered, and Cyrenaica had also defected to Octavian. Antony left the fleet at the desolate, sunbaked town of Paraetonium on Egypt's western border, there to lick his wounds for a time in private.

Cleopatra sailed on to Alexandria, anxious to head off trouble: If news of the defeat at Actium had already reached her enemies, they might be emboldened to revolt. She decked her flagship with garlands and made a brave show of returning in triumph. Then she feverishly began gathering her wealth and firming up her alliances

in the Levant with the aim of rebuilding the fleet and the army. Accepting defeat was simply not in her nature. She never gave up.

Antony proved less resilient. He eventually returned to Alexandria—but not to the palace. Rather, he closeted himself inside a rude lodge on the harbor, naming it the Timonium after the famous misanthrope Timon of Athens. It was a typically dramatic display of his despair, but he soon tired of it. He returned to Cleopatra, who welcomed him with a new round of banquets and parties. The Inimitable Livers society was revived, but renamed—doubtless by Antony—Those Who Will Die Together.

Cleopatra, however, had no intention of dying if she could help it. Maybe a world empire ruled by Rome and Egypt was no longer possible, but she would hold Egypt if she could, and if that failed, she would use her treasure to found a new kingdom elsewhere. She had in mind India, a land beyond the reach of the Romans.

In furtherance of this aim, she undertook the difficult task of

This block from the Hermonthis Temple, lying upside down, is the only fragment still bearing the cartouche of Cleopatra, *left*. Also carved into the block is a falcon crowned with a solar disk and holding between its wings the circular *shem* sign, a symbol of eternity. The line running through the circle is part of a *was* scepter, emblematic of power. *Below:* This Byzantine mosaic from St. John's Church in Jordan identifies in Greek lettering the portrayed city as Alexandria. Such architectural elements as crosses, however, typify the artist's era rather than that of ancient Alexandria.

transporting most of her fleet overland to the Red Sea and having even more ships built on its shores. If Octavian marched against her from the west, she could have Egypt's treasury loaded onto these vessels and escape with her children to the east. But this plan, too, was thwarted. The Nabataean Arabs, chafing under Egyptian rule, burned the ships.

For Cleopatra, who had once aspired to rule an empire mightier than Alexander's, only two ambitions remained: to secure the throne of Egypt for Caesarion, and to die like a queen.

In 30 B.C., Cleopatra and Antony staged a festival to celebrate Caesarion's coming of age. The boy, now sixteen, was thus acknowledged as a man and as king of Egypt, no matter what happened to his mother. During these festivities a Roman rite of passage was held for Antony's eldest son, fourteen-year-old Antyllus, who had joined his father in Greece before Actium. The rituals were part of Cleopatra's preparations for the end. Octavian was not yet at Alexandria's doorstep, but he soon would be.

Rather than pursue Antony and Cleopatra after Actium, Octavian had returned to Italy to quell unrest among the army veterans who were demanding their customary retirement rights of farmland and money. Octavian made them soothing promises that he was confident he could keep: There was plenty of money in Egypt.

In the summer of 30 B.C., he sailed to Phoenicia. There he was met by three envoys from Egypt. Two brought Cleopatra's royal insignia and a large bribe, along with the message that she was willing to abdicate if Octavian would allow her children to rule in Egypt. He kept the insignia and the money but made no promises. The third messenger, Antyllus himself, brought more money, along with Antony's plea that he be allowed to retire to private life. Octavian didn't deign to reply.

ΑΛΕΞΑΝΔΡΙΑ

Soon the Roman army was closing in on Alexandria. Pelusium, on Egypt's eastern border, had fallen. There had been no help in that quarter from Antony's erstwhile ally in Judea; Herod, like so many others, had gone over to Octavian. In the west, the Romans were in the suburb of Canopus. Cleopatra had said good-bye to her beloved Caesarion, sending him east with his tutor.

In Alexandria, next to the Temple of Isis, Cleopatra had nearly finished building a mortuary temple, intended for her worship after her death. Into this structure she now moved as much as she could of Egypt's portable wealth: gold, silver, jewels, and rare spices. She also brought firewood. She would use the treasure to bargain with Octavian if she could; if she couldn't, she would burn it.

With Octavian at the city gates, messages began to fly back and forth; clearly, Octavian knew that the treasure was in jeopardy, and it must be saved at all costs. He wrote to Cleopatra, promising rather vaguely to deal fairly with her and suggesting that all would go well if she had Antony killed. The proposal must have elicited some mordant humor in the queen. After Actium, Herod had suggested to Antony that he should kill Cleopatra, thereby effecting a reconciliation with Octavian. Antony had rejected the idea out of hand, as Cleopatra did now. She had loved him, after all, passionately and for years—not with the worship she'd given Caesar, but as the flawed yet admirable man that he was. She would not betray him. And, despite past waywardness, he had loved her. Since their reunion at Antioch, he had proved time after time that she was the grand passion of his life.

He was about to prove it again. He sent a message to Octavian, promising to kill himself if Cleopatra would be spared. There was no reply.

On their last night together, the couple dined exceptionally well before retiring, knowing that the coming day would decide their fate at last. The streets of Alexandria were quiet—except, it was said, for a strange and phantom music. There was a well-known legend in the East that the gods abandon a city before its fall. On this night, faint sounds of flutes and cymbals supposedly disturbed the peace of Alexandria, as though some joyous procession were passing invisibly

through the city and away. This was, some people believed, Dionysus deserting Antony.

At dawn on August 1, 30 B.C., Antony took his place at the head of the remnants of his army, and the remaining Egyptian ships moved out of Alexandria's harbor toward Octavian's fleet. Cleopatra may have watched from her window, as she had so long ago during the Alexandrian War. If so, she would have seen her ships raise their oars in salute to Octavian as they went over to his side. Antony's cavalry also deserted, and the small infantry was easily scattered in defeat. Cleopatra fled to her mortuary temple, taking with her one of her eunuchs and her two most trusted serving women, Charmion and Iras.

Antony returned to the palace to hear from Cleopatra's servants that the queen had killed herself. Presumably, she had left this message so that he would commit suicide too, and he resolved to do so. He handed his sword to his servant Eros and asked him to run him through. Unable to do it, Eros killed himself instead. Antony then fell on his own sword and was mortally wounded.

Assuming him already dead, Cleopatra sent her secretary, Diomedes, to bring his body to her. It was from Diomedes that Antony learned the queen was still alive. He was carried to her temple. Its door was barricaded by now, but the three women inside were able to hoist Antony up by ropes through a window high on one side of the unfinished structure.

He died in Cleopatra's arms. His last words to her told much of what he truly was, regardless of the allure the East had held for him. She was not to grieve, he said. He was a Roman, conquered by a Roman.

When news of Antony's death reached Octavian, he dispatched one of his men, Proculeius, in great haste to the temple. Octavian feared the queen might kill herself, or burn the treasure, or both. No less than the wealth, he coveted Cleopatra herself, to parade her in chains behind his chariot in triumph through the streets of Rome.

Speaking through a grate, Proculeius tried to persuade Cleopatra to leave her mausoleum. She would do so, she said, only with Octavian's assurance that her children would rule in Egypt.

The tragedy of Mark Antony's death was a fitting counterpoint to the exuberant fullness of his life with Cleopatra. Plutarch describes movingly how the dying general, "covered all over with blood," was hoisted up through a window into the queen's mortuary temple, where *"she laid him on the bed, tearing all her clothes, which she spread upon him; and beating her breasts with her hands, lacerating herself, and disfiguring her own face with the blood from his wounds, she called him her lord, her husband, her emperor, and seemed to have pretty nearly forgotten all her own evils, she was so intent upon his misfortunes."*

Above: Antony, in this detail from Francesco Trevisani's *The Banquet of Cleopatra and Mark Antony.*

Proculeius replied obliquely that she should trust Octavian. That was hardly likely, but as they talked, Proculeius spotted the window through which Antony's body had been hauled. He called in two men to talk to the queen and her servants, thus keeping them occupied while he scaled the wall and entered through the window. When Cleopatra saw him, she drew a dagger and tried to stab herself, but Proculeius wrenched the knife away and took her captive.

She was put under house arrest in her own palace, and there began her last war with Octavian: his fight to keep her alive, her fight to die.

She won permission from him to give Antony a suitable burial, and during the ceremony she mourned him after the fashion of the women of Egypt, tearing her hair and her clothes and clawing her breasts in grief. Afterward she refused food for a time, hoping to starve herself to death. Octavian sent word that unless she began eating, he would kill the three of her children who still remained in Egypt. She ate.

Cleopatra knew now that her only hope lay in convincing Octavian that she meant to live.

At last he visited her in person, finding her disheveled, but in reasonable health. She gave him a list of all her treasures, but a servant whispered to him that she had left out some valuable bits of jewelry. Cleopatra began beating the servant and crying to Octavian that she'd meant only to save some gifts by which she might endear herself to the women in his family. It was a good show; Octavian believed that she would try to survive.

The courage and pride with which Cleopatra met death won grudging praise even from some of her Roman enemies. The poet Horace, for instance, who had called her "a crazy queen" bent on toppling Rome, also wrote this of her: "With fortitude she handled fierce snakes, her corporeal frame drank in their venom: resolved for death, she was brave indeed. She was no docile woman but truly scorned to be taken away in her enemy's ships, deposed, to an overweening Triumph." Painting by artist Reginald Arthur.

Around August 12, three days before she was due to depart for Rome with Octavian, she asked to visit Antony's tomb, and permission was granted. There she placed flowers on his sarcophagus and kissed it, then returned to the palace to bathe and dine. Iras and Charmion attended her. During the meal, a peasant was allowed into her apartments with a basket of figs. She had managed somehow to arrange for this gift. Her guards, inspecting the basket, remarked on how large and succulent the figs looked. They didn't see what lay beneath them.

The guards left, and Cleopatra opened the basket. The figs stirred and fell away, and there lifted into view the flat head of a cobra, the deliverer whose bite would send her, a queen of Egypt, to the immortal care of the gods.

About the same time, Octavian was opening a letter from the queen. It contained only one request: that she be buried beside Antony. He sent soldiers hurrying to her rooms.

They threw open the doors to find Cleopatra, last pharaoh of Egypt, laid out on a golden bed, attired in her royal robes and jewels. Iras lay dead at her mistress's feet. Charmion, dying, was trying to adjust the diadem on the dead queen's forehead.

One of the soldiers, outraged, screamed at the servant, "Was this well done of your lady, Charmion?"

With effort, she lifted her head to meet this Roman's eyes, as Cleopatra would have wished.

"Extremely well," she said, "as became the daughter of so many noble rulers."

Chapter VI

DISCOVERY

Mercifully, Cleopatra did not live to hear the one report that might have shattered her relentless will: Caesarion was dead. His tutor had betrayed him to Octavian, and Octavian, reasoning that too many Caesars was not a good thing, ordered him killed. He dealt with Antony's son Antyllus in the same way.

Cleopatra's remaining children, the twins and little Ptolemy, were raised by Mark Antony's widow, Cleopatra's archrival Octavia, probably with the Roman woman's customary kindness. None would ever rule in Egypt. The dynasty of the Ptolemies, the last pharaohs, had ended with the death of its greatest queen.

Antony's line would continue to play a role in history, although an appalling one.

A diver looks on as a granite head, identified as an effigy of Cleopatra's nemesis Octavian, rises into the sunlight after countless centuries in Alexandrian waters. Although Goddio's team temporarily raised some exceptional finds for study, all were later replaced on the seabed pending a decision on their final fate.

Through descendants of his two daughters by Octavia, he would become the ancestor of two of the most maniacal of Rome's imperial lunatics, Caligula and Nero.

Octavian annexed Egypt shortly after Cleopatra's death. He would go on to become Caesar Augustus, the first and greatest of the Roman emperors, and he would rule long and well until his death at the age of seventy-seven, holding absolute power while never ceasing to claim that he had preserved the republic. Such hypocrisy notwithstanding, he ended Rome's incessant civil wars, expanded and consolidated the empire, brought it stability and prosperity, knitted its far-flung lands together with roadways that exist to this day, and began a building program that would transform Rome into a magnificent city.

He also instituted valuable and lasting governmental and administrative reforms, and as the patron of such writers as Virgil, Horace, Ovid, and Livy, he oversaw an unparalleled flowering of Roman culture. In short, Octavian was the right man, at the right time, for Rome.

History, then, would move swiftly past Cleopatra's death. An era was ending, and one beginning. But what of beautiful Alexandria, her dynastic capital?

Time ages cities, just as it does people, but unlike their flesh-and-blood inhabitants, great metropolises sometimes grow stronger as they get older. The death of Cleopatra and the switch to Roman rule did not weaken Alexandria. In fact, full integration into the Roman Empire, the biggest free-trade kingdom of the ancient world, brought a new surge of commercial energy and an increase in the population.

Yet there was a price to pay for rising affluence. Under the Ptolemies, Alexandria had at least been a seat of power, however despotically it may have been exercised. Now, the city's fate lay in the hands of remote rulers in Rome, a three-week journey across the Mediterranean.

For the most part, these distant authorities were happy enough to let Alexandria go its own cosmopolitan way, just as long as Roman interests were served. The rich agricultural lands surrounding the Nile became the granary of the empire, and the main concern of the emperors was simply to see that the grain fleets that fed their people arrived regularly. Occasionally, however, circumstances caused them to intervene directly in Alexandria's affairs, sometimes in horrifying ways.

Today, the Port of Alexandria, previous spread, shows no visible signs of the ancient land masses that once defined it. The coastline, shaped in a semicircle, features long modern breakwaters that protect it from the sea on both east and west sides. Below: Ancient glass fragments from the Roman period found in the royal harbor of Antirhodos Island

One of the city's darkest hours was during the reign of the unstable emperor Caracalla, who, as one ancient text has it, ordered a massacre of all its young men. Another time of trial occurred in the third century when, in the wake of civil disturbances, the authorities closed down the Museum, Alexandria's great international center of learning, and ordered the destruction of the city wall that is thought by some to have extended beyond the Royal Quarter and enclosed the entire city. Over the ensuing years the sands of the surrounding scrubland invaded the depopulated area where the Ptolemies' palaces had once stood, and by the following century that part of the city was little more than desert, though the other quarters prospered and the port was still crowded with shipping.

Further change came with the adoption of Christianity as the Empire's official religion in the fourth century A.D., which led to the destruction of the Serapeion. This temple, dedicated to the pagan god Serapis, was described as the world's finest building after the Capitol in Rome itself; it also contained what was left of Alexandria's world-famous Library, which had gone up in flames. The city gained new status, though, as the patriarchate of Egypt's native Coptic church, but the cosmopolitan and cultural luster Alexandria had enjoyed in earlier times was now just a memory.

When the Empire was divided between Rome and Byzantium in A.D. 395—at last fulfilling Cleopatra's dream of an empire with capitals in both West and East—Alexandria found itself in the Byzantine camp, thereby surviving the fall of Rome to barbarians soon afterward. The next great upheaval came in the seventh century when, after a fourteen-month siege, the city was taken by Arab invaders.

A Despot's Wrath

Fragments of Greek dedications inscribed on the panels of a number of red-granite columns found on Antirhodos point to the reign of one of Alexandria's most despotic rulers—Caracalla, son of Septimus Severus and ruler of Egypt between A.D. 198 and 217.

Portrayed by one ancient source as a charming, sensitive, and kind child, Caracalla had by adulthood sought refuge in military pursuits, traveling rough with his soldiers and taking every opportunity to show off his own toughness. Shortly after coming to power jointly with his cultured, level-headed brother Geta, he arranged Geta's murder, seizing sole power.

The general dislike of him as an adult is clear in several ancient sources. Roman historian Dio Cassius paints a portrait of a shifty, impulsive, and stubborn man who was impaired both mentally and physically. Herodian saw Caracalla as harsh, immature, and violent. Both describe a ghastly massacre that he ordered on the citizens of Alexandria.

Though both historians offer a variation on the story, they agree that Caracalla's latent aversion to the pleasure-loving Alexandrians turned to hatred when word reached him that local satirists were making fun of his unprepossessing appearance, his self-comparisons to the likes of Alexander the Great and Achilles, and his blood-stained rise to power. When he arrived in Alexandria with his army, he showed no sign of hostile intentions, and the city gave him a warm welcome. Then, without warning, he ordered the massacre of a large number of citizens.

In Dio Cassius' account, Caracalla visited the city, receiving a number of dignitaries with favor as they carried sacred objects in a procession to meet him. He then put them all to death and ordered a massacre that lasted for several days. No record of the numbers killed was kept. According to Dio Cassius, Caracalla himself grimly told the Roman Senate that the casualty figures were unimportant; all Alexandrians deserved to die.

Herodian's version describes Caracalla attending a number of assemblies and feasts. Then, noticing a tremendous gathering of people, he issued an edict calling for all Alexandrian youths to gather on an esplanade to be inspected for an infantry that Caracalla was to create in honor of Alexander the Great. As family and friends watched in horror, Caracalla ordered his troops to slay the young men and to slaughter as many others as they could. The carnage was so great, Herodian writes, that the nearby river water was reddened with the blood.

A damaged papyrus found in modern times at Hermopolis, north of Thebes, may provide contemporary clues to the actual event. The document, which appears to be a record of a hearing over which Caracalla presided, mentions a riot, possibly provoked by the wealthy classes, that resulted in the damage of statuary commissioned by Caracalla. In response, the tyrant ordered the death of those involved, including the Egyptian prefect, and called for a massacre to quell any further revolt.

Whatever incited this bloodthirsty emperor to wreak vengeance on the Alexandrians, the discovery of the inscriptions on Antirhodos nearly two millennia later serves as an inescapable reminder of the cost of attracting a despot's wrath.

Left: A quartz monzonite portrait of the Emperor Caracalla (circa A.D. 211–217) found at the Temple of Isis, Koptos, Egypt.

Its future would lie with Islam, though a substantial Christian minority has continued to live there. The conquerors treated Alexandria generously, but it lost its political preeminence when a new capital was established on a site near present-day Cairo.

Even as the city was buffeted by political and religious forces, its layout was dramatically altered by events that went almost unnoted in the historical record. Then as now, the eastern Mediterranean was seismically active, and a series of earthquakes, some accompanied by tidal waves, hit the north African coast in the vicinity of the city, causing catastrophic collapse of the land into the sea. One particularly devastating shock is known to have struck on July 21, 365, and further tremors followed in the ensuing centuries. Islamic chronicles tell of another quake almost a thousand years later, in 1308, that caused the final toppling of the Pharos lighthouse.

Alexandria was invisibly vulnerable to natural calamity. The city lay on a geological fault line, near the juncture of two of the continent-sized tectonic plates that make up the subsurface of the Earth's crust—a circumstance that occasioned not only earthquakes but a gradual sinking of the land. Imperceptibly but inexorably, the African shelf on which Alexandria stood was forced downward beneath the European plate to its north, causing the whole coastal region to subside. Current evidence suggests that the littoral has sunk as much as twenty feet since Cleopatra's death, while sea levels have risen over the same period by another four or five feet. In a related development, the Canopic branch of the Nile, which in earlier times supplied Lake Mareotis on the city's landward side with fresh water, gradually silted up, becoming unnavigable by the thirteenth century. As a result of these geophysical changes, Alexandria's ancient shoreline gradually disappeared beneath the waters of the East Port. The

In the foreground is a white-marble head of Antonia Minor, *left,* daughter of Mark Antony. Behind it can be seen the magnificent marble statue of a form of the Greek god Hermes. It is either a Ptolemaic king representing the god or the god himself.

Below: Identification of Antonia Minor was aided by hairstyle comparisons taken from other portraits of the period.

city's Greek rulers had chosen to build their palaces on the seafront, so the entire Royal Quarter of the Ptolemies disappeared.

In the long centuries of Islamic rule, under Arabs, Mamelukes, and Ottoman Turks, Alexandria's importance as a trading center steadily declined, and by the beginning of the nineteenth century the city had reached the low point of its fortunes, reduced to the status of a sleepy Mediterranean backwater with a population of only six thousand people. Yet if the city itself had fallen into neglect, its last queen had not been forgotten. In Europe the Renaissance had reawakened interest in the Hellenistic heritage, and generations of educated individuals across the continent had, like Caesar and Antony before them, fallen under Cleopatra's spell. The English playwright William Shakespeare read her story in the *Lives* of the Greek biographer Plutarch and then made it his own in his tragedy of *Antony and Cleopatra.*

Inevitably, interest in Cleopatra inspired interest in her city. Thus, even at a time when Alexandria's fortunes were at a low ebb, scholars were already turning their minds to reconstructing, at least on paper, its past glories. The trouble was that, for the most part, they had very little evidence to go on. No maps of the city had survived from antiquity, only descriptions in books. And many of the buildings themselves now lay hidden under the sea.

The scholarly investigators did the best they could. From the sixteenth century on, they made attempts at outlining the old city, basing their estimates for the most part on a description by the Greek geographer Strabo, who had visited Alexandria shortly after Cleopatra's death. But even though Strabo wrote clearly of its individual buildings and general layout, scholars disagreed about the way the features fitted together.

STRABO'S ALEXANDRIA

Born in 64 B.C. in what is now eastern Turkey, Strabo was a globetrotter whose expeditions took him from Armenia to Italy and from the Black Sea to the borders of Ethiopia. He produced a now-lost forty-seven-volume history of Rome as well as the seventeen-volume *Geography* for which he is best known today.

Although he borrowed extensively from other authors to describe many of the places his works covered, the section on Alexandria was based on first-hand knowledge. Scholars believe that he visited the city around 27 B.C., arriving in the entourage of the second Roman prefect to rule Alexandria after Cleopatra VII's death. The excerpt below, taken from *Geography,* provided the only information on which earlier cartographers could reconstruct the submerged city.

"In the Great Harbour at the entrance, on the right hand, are the island and the tower Pharos, and on the other hand are the reefs and also the promontory Lochias, with a royal palace upon it; and on sailing into the harbour one comes, on the left, to the inner royal palaces, which are continuous with those on Lochias and have groves and numerous lodges painted in various colours. Below these lies the harbour that was dug by the hand of man and is hidden from view, the private property of the kings, as also Antirhodos, an isle lying off the artificial harbour, which has both a royal palace and a small harbour. They so called it as being a rival of Rhodes. Above the artificial harbour lies the theatre; then the Poseidium—an elbow, as it were, projecting from the Emporium, as it is called, and containing a temple of Poseidon. To this elbow of land Antony added a mole projecting still farther, into the middle of a harbour, and on the extremity of it built a royal lodge which he called Timonium...."

Below: This grid of the ancient city of Alexandria was, in part, based on the earlier reconstruction efforts undertaken by astronomer and engineer Mahmoud Bey, who in 1866 produced what was considered the most reliable map of the time.

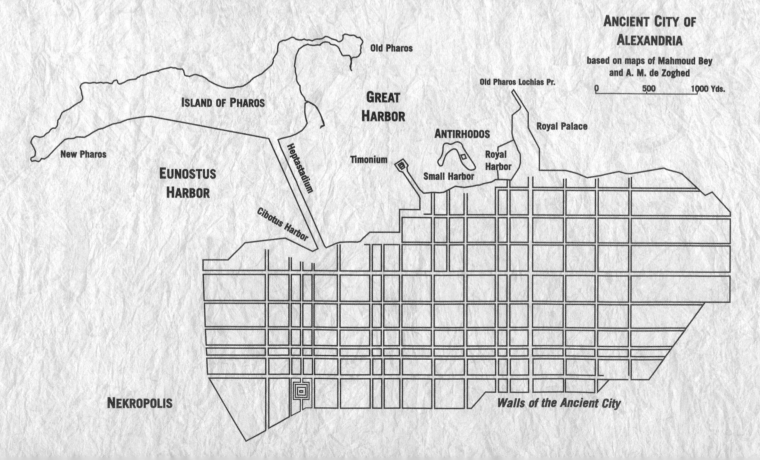

ANCIENT CITY OF ALEXANDRIA

based on maps of Mahmoud Bey and A. M. de Zoghed

0   500   1000 Yds.

Old Pharos

GREAT HARBOR

Old Pharos Lochias Pr.

ISLAND OF PHAROS

Royal Palace

ANTIRHODOS

New Pharos

Timonium

Royal Harbor

Heptastadium

Small Harbor

EUNOSTUS HARBOR

Cibotus Harbor

NEKROPOLIS

Walls of the Ancient City

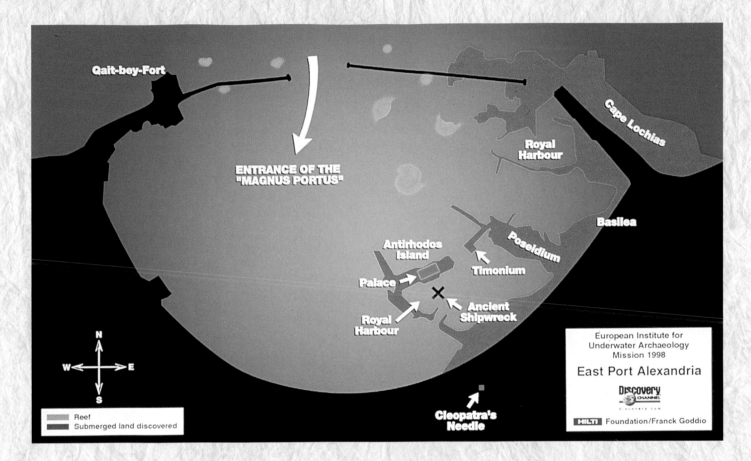

The submerged topography of Alexandria's Magnus Portus (Great Port) as surveyed using modern technology. Remapped areas include Cape Lochias (near what is known today as Cape Silsileh); the walled city around the eastern part of the port; the peninsula (referred to by Strabo as the Poseidium and the site of Mark Antony's Timonium); the island of Antirhodos; the ancient coastline marked by the remains of the Inner Palaces, or basileia; and the reefs, which had in ancient times posed a challenge to those guiding their boats into the port.

Most dramatic is the placement of Antirhodos and the peninsula.

Earlier maps have mistakenly placed the island to the east of the peninsula and greatly reduced the area of Cape Lochias.

The problem came to the fore in 1865, when France's ruler, Napoleon III, asked the Egyptian authorities to provide a definitive map of ancient Alexandria for a book he was planning on Julius Caesar's African campaign. Eager to gratify a foreign head of state, they entrusted the job of drawing up the plan to an astronomer and engineer named Mahmoud Bey (later knighted and known as Mahmoud El Falaki). He undertook the task conscientiously, tracing all surviving mainland vestiges of the Hellenistic city and even digging some trenches in an attempt to verify its layout. For the submerged quarter, however, he could only rely on conjecture. Mahmoud Bey's work was to serve as the basis for most subsequent reconstructions—but it would prove flawed.

The fact was that Mahmoud Bey and his successors simply didn't have the technological means to investigate the sunken city, even though its remains were tantalizingly close, lying within a few hundred yards of the shore. Further progress had to wait for advances in the developing science of underwater archaeology.

In Mahmoud Bey's time, submarine investigation could only be undertaken in cumbersome diving suits, or bells. A great leap forward came with the development of aqualung equipment. Although the earliest working model was patented in 1828, it took over a century of improvement to arrive at the basis of the modern SCUBA system (Self-Contained Underwater Breathing Apparatus) with a perfected breathing valve developed by Emile Gagnan and Jacques Yves Cousteau in 1946. SCUBA equipment gave the users freedom to roam the seabed at will. Wide-ranging underwater exploration was at last a practical possibility.

Early attempts to put this equipment to use produced some dramatic results. In the 1960s an Egyptian diver,

Found in the small, private harbor of Antirhodos, this plate, probably Aegean, dates back to the 1st century B.C. and is a later variation on what was once a common Hellenistic shape.

Kemal Abu El Saadat, discovered two joining pieces of an enormous statue near the site of the Pharos lighthouse. Over twenty-three feet in length, it was the statue of a Ptolemaic queen represented as the goddess Isis. Subsequently El Saadat made exploratory dives in the inner harbor, but he lacked the means to undertake a thorough survey. Then a new and highly resourceful player appeared on the scene: In the 1980s Franck Goddio would begin unlocking the secrets of the sunken city.

A French citizen, Goddio is the grandson of the late Eric de Bisschop, the inventor of the modern catamaran, and the spirit of maritime adventure has always run in his blood. He began his career in a very different field, however, working as a government financial adviser in Vietnam, Cambodia, and Laos at the time of the Vietnam War. Subsequently he helped create the Saudi Fund for Development, a government institution that granted loans to developing countries, and managed the Fund's activities in Africa. Not until he was in his mid-thirties did Goddio—literally—take the plunge into marine exploration.

Goddio got an early taste of its thrills in 1984, when he joined a leading French diver, Jacques Dumas, on a project to explore the wreck of *L'Orient,* the flagship of Napoleon Bonaparte's Egyptian fleet, which was sunk in 1798 at the Battle of the Nile. It was Dumas who first told him of the submersion of ancient Alexandria and of the archaeological treasures that presumably still lay hidden beneath the waves. Goddio had other projects in mind at the time, but the story intrigued him. Over the next six years he read all the available material on the city and its fate.

Some of the expedition participants gather around a priest statue, one of the team's most prized discoveries. First row, left to right: Roland Savoye, Jean-Claude Roubaud, Franck Goddio; second row: Mohamed Abd El Hamid, (statue), Ibrahim Darwish (co-director of the project with Goddio), Emily Teeter; third row: Fernand Pereira, Bernard Camier, Mustafa El Dissouki, Eric Smith, Alaa El Din Mahrous, Stephane Brousse, unidentified Egyptian naval officer, Patrice Sandrin, Georges Brocot.

Following spread: Divers carefully handle the remains of an Egyptian wine amphora which dates between the 1st and 3rd centuries A.D. and is believed to have been produced in the Mareotic region, southwest of Alexandria.

Like previous seekers, he relied heavily on Strabo for information, and before long the Greek writer's description of the lost city was firmly implanted in his mind. Strabo spoke of a promontory, Cape Lochias, where a royal palace had stood, with more palaces adjoining it on the mainland shoreline. Facing them was a harbor, "dug by the hand of man and hidden from view," which was the private property of the kings.

So too was a small offshore island, Antirhodos, "which has both a palace and a small harbour." Completing the Royal Quarter was an "elbow of land" extending out into the port; this promontory was known as the Poseidium, since a temple to the Greek sea god Poseidon, popular in Alexandria, had once stood there. Here, Strabo reported, Mark Antony built a lodge when he returned to the city after his crushing defeat at Actium. Called the Timonium and sited at the end of a breakwater, it briefly served as Antony's retreat from the world.

In 1987 Goddio—by now fully committed to a career of submarine exploration—set up the Institut Européen d'Archéologie Sous-Marine (IEASM) and embarked on an ambitious program of investigating far-flung wrecks. He met with quick success, winning worldwide media attention for his work on the *San Diego,* a Spanish galleon lost off the Philippines in the year 1600. But he had not forgotten Alexandria, and a chance encounter in 1990 finally set him on the hunt for its secrets. Goddio was then visiting Egypt with a deputation from the French Ministry of Foreign Affairs. At an official luncheon, he was seated next to H. E. Farouk Hosni, the Egyptian minister of culture, who listened enthusiasti-

Onboard the *Oceanex*, Franck Goddio and a colleague chart the progress of the survey on a computer screen. Details of all finds such as the vessel shown on the previous spread were logged in along with details of the exact location where they were discovered—vital information for determining the function of submerged buildings.

cally as Goddio described his long-held hopes of investigating the East Port and who encouraged him to seek the necessary permissions. Goddio was heartened by his support and decided to forge ahead.

The task in front of him was daunting. The East Port was nearly as big as New York's Central Park, more than eight hundred acres; mapping its bed was going to be an arduous and time-consuming project. In addition, the area was now a military zone, and many different agencies had to give their approval before the project could go ahead.

With the necessary permits in hand, the mission was ready to proceed by 1992. Goddio decided that the first step would be a general survey, aimed at finding the most interesting sites; detailed examination would come later. To conduct the survey, he packed three tons of electronic equipment onto the *Kaimiloa,* a research vessel built to his specifications. (*Kaimiloa,* Hawaiian for "beyond the farthest horizons," was the name of Goddio's grandfather's pioneering catamaran.)

For three months the *Kaimiloa* crisscrossed the port's murky waters, dragging in its wake three torpedo-shaped objects, each of them painted bright yellow. These towfish, as they were called, contained state-of-the-art electronic equipment that included nuclear magnetic resonance magnetometers developed by France's Atomic Energy Commission. These extremely sensitive instruments were able to produce a magnetic profile of the seabed, detecting any magnetic anomalies that might indicate the presence of objects of possible archaeological significance.

While the magnetometers proved valuable, their performance was impaired by the amount of background interference from the modern city; even trams on the waterfront disturbed the readings. More information came from side-scan sonar devices, which transmitted micropulses of sound through the water in fan-shaped beams. Bouncing off any obstructions in their path, the pulses returned as echoes that, when electronically processed, served to build up a sonograph or "sound picture" of the seabed. At the same time, bathymeters measured the water depth to create a three-dimensional picture of the harbor bottom. Finally the task was completed; the entire port had been covered. Then came the next stage—analyzing and integrating all the information. The team's computers went to work, weaving together the first scientific images of the Ptolemies' lost city, after which Goddio and his chief technical collaborators gathered to study the results. Although the images produced by the computers were vague and imprecise, there was something decidedly magical in seeing a dead city appear on a screen in ghostly outline.

The computers showed the search area from the top down. The surface level was, of course, a blank, but evocative shapes began to loom into view just a little below. At eighteen feet, large-scale structures could be seen—an ancient harbor, perhaps? A little deeper, a second haven appeared, this one in the lee of Cape Lochias at the eastern part of the port, where Strabo had placed the private mooring of the Ptolemies. Lower still, other mysteries presented themselves: first an amorphous shape

This small Egyptian cooking pot, dating between the 1st and 2nd centuries A.D., remains remarkably intact after almost two millennia under the harbor waters. Pottery finds proved relatively easy to date, since over the years the scientific community has built up a comprehensive database of artifact information that assists archaeologists in their comparative analysis studies.

resembling an island—Antirhodos?—then a promontory, maybe the "elbow of land" where a temple to Poseidon may have once stood. Farther down, the screen blurred into electronic haze. This was seafloor level, at which the computer could register only confusion.

The information the survey provided was fascinating, for there were undoubtedly man-made structures under the sea and the team now had a good idea of where to look for them. But the task of mapping the sunken city had only begun. The hard part lay ahead—fleshing out the details. It was now time for divers to go down in person for close-up inspections of the configurations.

Setting up this second stage of the investigation required more permits as well as financial support. Through the permission of the Egyptian Supreme Council of Antiquities and the sponsorship of the Hilti Foundation, a Liechtenstein-based charitable trust, Franck Goddio was able to proceed with assembling the personnel and equipment that would be needed to continue his study of the port. By June 1996, he had brought together a group of IEASM experts and a number of archaeologists from the Council's Department of Underwater Archaeology, including its director, Ibrahim Darwish, who became Goddio's project codirector. The *Oceanex,* a ninety-foot-long ship freshly acquired from the Alexandria naval dockyards, was to serve as the base of operations, supported by two additional vessels.

The survey of the large area was designed to be comprehensive. The divers had to explore a large area of seabed, taking

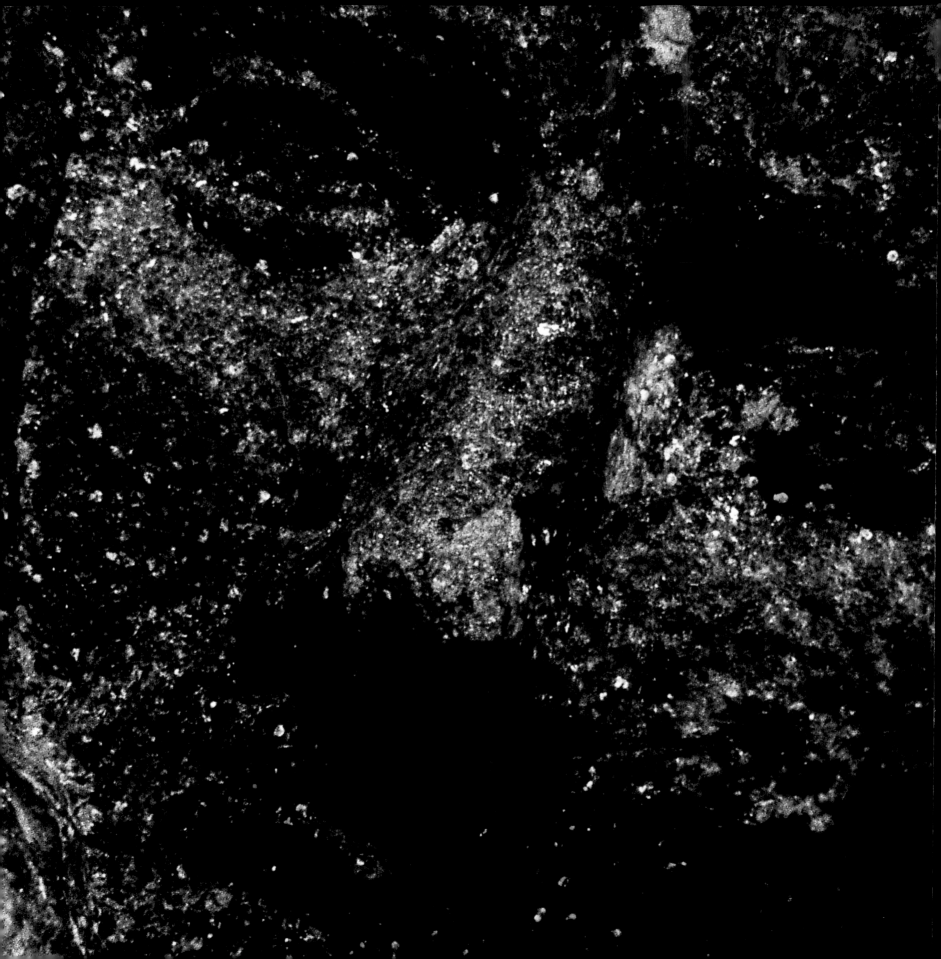

In this dramatic close-up, *left,* a strongly chiseled mouth, long nose, and deep-set eyes all contribute to the solemn expression on the face of a priest statue discovered on Antirhodos.

Above: Near the base of the peninsula, the IEASM team uncovered what they consider to be a rare find: a portion of statuary in the shape of a coiled serpent. No other such sculptural representation of a serpent exists. Associated with the serpent image was Agathodaïmon, a popular, local deity responsible for the prosperity and well being of Alexandria and its inhabitants.

measurements, marking out the contours of submerged structures, investigating any unusual objects, and fixing the position of each find with the greatest possible precision. Goddio began by investigating a large, island-like mass near the center of the port, what he thought could be Strabo's Antirhodos. For a week the divers concentrated their efforts there. Wearing protective dry suits and hoods to shield themselves from the sewage that contaminated the port waters, they made two daily dives of an average duration of one hundred minutes each. They found nothing but bare rock. It soon became apparent that the outcrop was actually a large, barren reef.

Goddio then determined to try a different tack. This time the team was dispatched in a direction that corresponded to an area on the electronic rendering that registered another massive form. A breakthrough came when diver Daniel Visnikar surfaced to stammer out excitedly that he had found amphorae—ancient storage jars of a distinctive shape—near what looked like a sunken jetty. Better yet, he had seen signs of paving stones.

Further investigation of the land mass soon indicated that it was not connected to the now-submerged seashore. According to Strabo's ancient text, there was only one island within the Great Port of Alexandria. Antirhodos had been located.

The divers then began tracing the outline of a four-hundred-yard-long promontory strewn with broken sections of pink-granite columns. (Surrealistically, the remains of a WWII British light bomber rested on the pavement beside the fractured columns.) As data accumulated on the submerged island, its shape

Ticketed for identification purposes, two clay jars lie on the harbor bed where they were abandoned many centuries ago. Known as amphorae, the two-handled containers served as standard measures, each holding nearly seven U.S. gallons, and could store a variety of food items, including wine, olive oil, and olives.

was gradually revealed. It took roughly the form of a capital T, with its main branch running parallel with the shore southwest to northeast. A northern crosspiece pointing toward the mouth of the port seemed to serve as a breakwater, and a third branch, running northwest to southeast, featured a small harbor. What held great promise at that point were the columns, blocks, and paving stones on both the main and southern branches, for they suggested monumental structures of some kind.

While examining the eastern tip of the island, the divers came upon something wholly unexpected: submerged ancient wooden structures, including stakes and planks. Calibrated carbon-14 dating placed the wood at approximately 400 B.C. (±40 B.C.)—well before Alexander the Great officially founded Alexandria. Evidently the remains of a jetty, they strongly suggested a native Egyptian settlement in pre-Greek times. Ancient records do mention a guardpost named Rhakotis (or Rhacotes) in the area, but little else is known. These signs of human activity indicated a more substantial community once existed in the area than scholars had previously imagined, a provocative discovery indeed.

In all, some 3,550 separate dives made in 1996 turned up traces of ancient quays, statue fragments, and hieroglyphic inscriptions. At a press conference that November, Goddio felt confident enough to announce to the world that the royal city of the Ptolemies had at last been found.

A diver delicately removes the encrustations off the monumental granite head identified as that of Caesar Augustus, shown wearing a nemes, or royal headdress. The absence of a uraeus—the serpentine headband worn by Egyptian pharaohs— helped identify the image as that of a Roman asserting sovereignty over Egypt without laying claim to the divine kingship.

Its very shape an icon of ancient Egypt, a sphinx looms enigmatically in the dirty green waters of the port, where pollution sometimes limited the range of visibility to little more than an arm's-length. In all, four sphinxes were found in the first two years of exploration. All were of similar dimensions, ranging from four to six feet in length. As images of regal strength, sphinxes normally bore the portrait of the reigning monarch. In this case, the faces of two of the sphinxes were too badly eroded to permit any identification. The other two, however, found together on the western shore of Antirhodos, have been classified as late Ptolemies, one of them probably Cleopatra's father, Ptolemy XII, Auletes.

During the following seasons, the hunt was pressed onward throughout the eastern part of the port, and as divers repeatedly slipped down into the undersea gloom, knowledge of the ancient city grew. In addition to surveying the submerged topography, the team carefully uncovered and recorded a tremendous amount of architectural and artifact evidence. For this, each diver was equipped with a compass strapped to his wrist and a small iron trowel to remove the encrustations, sometimes more than a foot thick, that cloaked most objects. Working on the seabed, the divers would painstakingly scrape the coating from a promising find, then sketch the object onto specially prepared paper. For ancient dikes or seawalls, they would carefully note the measurements to permit accurate mapping. When objects were buried deep in the Mediterranean mud, the divers used water dredges to vacuum up and displace the sediment that covered them.

To record placement, discoveries were marked by numbered orange buoys that bobbed up to the water's surface directly above. An ancillary team took readings on each buoy, using a space-age technology known as the Global Positioning System (GPS). The spot was then pinpointed on the master plan of the harbor that was stored on the ship's computer. As a variant on the GPS method, a device exclusively developed by Goddio allowed divers to take necessary positional readings from directly underwater.

As the mapping continued, Goddio became concerned about the condition of the ancient mainland shore. At one time the team had feared that the Corniche, a seafront boulevard constructed at the turn of the nineteenth century, might have done irreparable damage, covering all vestiges of the old palace

Identifiying a stone artifact such as this sphinx, *below,* believed to be of Ptolemy XII, often relied on conducting comparison studies of other ancient portraits that have been collected and catalogued.

Following spread: Members of the team look on intently as the sphinx emerges into the light of day for the first time in more than one and a half millennia.

quarter under landfill that was, in places, hundreds of feet deep. But discoveries made in 1997 allayed the team's worries. The shallows close to land yielded evidence of extensive limestone paving, red and gray granite blocks, and signs of a road, which meant that the ancient shoreline was still accessible.

One of the expedition's most tantalizing discoveries was made east of Antirhodos in the form of a major sunken promontory extending four hundred yards out from the ancient coastline into the harbor. Once mapped, its irregular outline simply could not be denied. It was clearly the "elbow of land" described by Strabo in his *Geography.* It featured four harbor structures and, like the coastline, significant remains at its base—granite and marble columns, fragments of ancient sarcophagi, and large blocks of stone that, conceivably, could have come from a temple of Poseidon.

But if the promontory was indeed Strabo's Poseidium, it followed that the site of Mark Antony's Timonium should lie at its tip. Divers in search of this retreat examined a two-hundred-yard-long embankment extending out from the end of the peninsula toward the entrance to the port, but the structure bore no signs of architectural remains and had instead probably served as a simple breakwater or pier.

Hope was revived, however, when a second promontory, built of limestone blocks, was discovered extending at a right angle westward from the base of the first. At its end, facing Antirhodos across a narrow channel, was a substantial paved limestone-and-mortar platform dotted with fallen granite columns. From this evidence, the site seemed the likeliest position of the Timonium.

PINPOINTING FINDS BY SATELLITE

The exploration of the entire East Port of Alexandria—an area the size of five hundred football fields—creates unique difficulties for underwater investigators. They not only have to find objects in the murky depths but also record their positions with the highest possible degree of accuracy. The problem has been compounded by the requirement to leave all findings in place on the seabed pending a final decision on their future.

To solve the problem, Franck Goddio's team turned to a technology originally developed for military use by the U.S. Department of Defense (DoD). The Global Positioning System (GPS) is a radio-navigation network of twenty-four NAVSTAR satellites devoted to transmitting signals globally around the clock, permitting land, sea, and airborne users to determine position, velocity, and time, under all weather conditions, anywhere in the world.

Situated eleven thousand miles above the Earth's surface, each GPS satellite completes two orbits daily, continuously transmitting its precise position and elevation. To determine a site's geographic location, a GPS receiver unit acquires the signal, then calculates its distance from the satellite by measuring the time difference between the signal's transmission and its receipt. Through a process known as triangulation, measurements are taken from three satellites to arrive at a three-dimensional location of longitude, latitude, and altitude. (A fourth satellite allows for the calculation of time.)

Since such pinpoint accuracy presents security issues, the DoD has equipped each satellite with a program that affects its civilian use. Called Selective Availability (SA), it directs a satellite to send out random error signals. To address this problem, the Goddio team employed Differential GPS (DGPS), a system designed to compensate for signal distortion. DGPS involves the use of a land-based reference GPS receiver station—in this case, a site on Fort Qaitbey on the western side of the port. Since the location of this reference point is already known, it serves as a constant, allowing the station to receive satellite signals and calculate their error factor. It formats this information into correction messages, which it relays to a radiobeacon antenna. The antenna then transmits the messages to the GPS user, who uses this offset, or differential, to correct his own signal readings.

In order to address the problem of limited visibility caused by the port's polluted waters, the team developed an innovative method of gathering DGPS data—a specially designed mobile receiving unit made watertight for undersea use. Nicknamed the "piano" because of its many key-like buttons, it is held in place manually over the find, while other team members position two floating antennae on the surface directly above to allow for an accurate reading.

The receiver's memory, which holds up to five hundred pieces of positioning data per dive, can be connected directly to a computer database, thus streamlining the task of recording location data. The system, whose land-based equivalent is now widely used in cartography, is accurate to within inches.

Right: Roland Savoye collects positioning data on a submerged sphinx using a waterproof mobile GPS receiver unit specially developed by the IEASM.

Left: A diagram showing DGPS at work. A reference station (A) receives satellite signals and uses its own location to calculate the error factor for each one. The data are formatted into correction messages which are then transmitted via radiobeacon (B) to the GPS user (C). These differential corrections are then applied to the GPS signals (D) received by the user, thus improving accuracy.

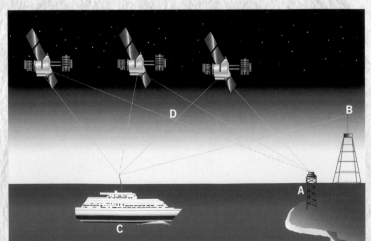

The finding of anonymous blocks of stone, columns, capitals, quays, and limestone pavings throughout the expedition area was, in itself, remarkable. But their importance resided in their relationship to what lay around them. A concentration of structural materials may, for example, indicate the presence of a fallen building.

When divers examined the area under the granite blocks and columns found on Antirhodos, they uncovered persuasive engineering evidence to support Strabo's description of a royal Ptolemaic structure that may have once stood on the island. At the island's widest point—the only place big enough to support a large structure—the team found a platform covering over sixty-four thousand square feet. Excavations performed on the site indicated that the platform was leveled with ancient mortar. Beneath it, wood coffer dams were discovered, preserved by the mortar. Analysis of the wood and the mortar's organic elements indicated a date of 250 B.C., with a margin of error of fifty years. This dating placed the platform—and the vanished structure built on it—firmly within the Ptolemaic era. How long this island structure stood, and when it fell, are questions as yet unanswered. It is possible that the palace was destroyed and subsequent structures were built on the site before the entire area was submerged.

What could perhaps help shed light on the construction history of the island and the rest of the port were the inscriptions surviving on the blocks, lintels, and columns found there. In keeping with the guidelines set forth by the Egyptian government, most of the discovered items were not to be raised. In order to provide scholars with access to the submerged text, moldings were made of the artifacts. As a result, Goddio's work benefited from the expertise of eminent scholars, such as Etienne

An aid to identifying this statue head as being that of Octavian was the regular and schematic arrangement of the hair fringe appearing from underneath the royal headdress. Such a style conforms to the convention recognized in Egyptian portraits of Roman emperors.

Bernand, Professor Emeritus at the French Universities, who studied the Greek and Latin inscriptions, and Jean Yoyotte of the College de France, who examined, among other artifacts, the Egyptian inscriptions.

Such epigraphic scholarship proved immensely valuable, for example, in the examination of several fragments of Greek dedication text engraved on the panels of shafts of red-granite columns found on the island. Collectively, they marked the remains as being from the early third-century reign of Caracalla, a notoriously unstable ruler. Their existence confirmed that construction on the island continued long after the Ptolemaic dynasty.

In addition to impressive construction remains, inscriptions, and various types of ceramics and pottery, divers also encountered many statuary pieces. The varied styles and locations of twelve of the largest and most significant found among the architectural rubble of four paved sites invited inquiries into the confluence of Greek, Roman, and Egyptian influences in ancient Alexandria.

On the southwestern bank of Antirhodos, divers found a magnificently preserved five-foot-tall gray granite statue of a fully cloaked priest carrying an effigy of Osiris-Canopus, a local popular version of the god Osiris. A find such as this is rare, according to Professor Françoise Dunand of the University of Strasbourg, since this type of statue is more commonly found outside Egypt. The presence of such an obviously religious work also suggests that a temple may have once stood at the site, one most likely dedicated to Osiris' wife and sister, the beloved goddess Isis. Although this statue dates closer to the second century A.D., it may rest on a previous temple site, one that could have adjoined a palace such as the one Strabo had noted on the island.

CANOPIC JARS

One of the most spectacular artworks to emerge from the seabed was a statue of a priest holding a human-headed jar. The find points up the reality behind a long-held scholarly misconception.

Greek legend tells of a man named Canopos (or Canobos) who served as a helmsman for Meneleus, the husband of Helen of Troy. During a trip to Egypt, Canopos fell victim to the bite of a serpent and was buried at the shore of the westernmost mouth of the Nile. He gave his name to a nearby town, known as Pegouti in Egyptian. The area was a flourishing port, often visited by Alexandrians as a pleasure resort.

According to Christian historian Rufinas, in *Historia Ecclesiastica II, XXVI*, the local representation of the god Osiris at this western branch of the Nile was in the form of a sacred jar

topped by a human head. The jar was not a ritual object, but merely a rendering of one of the aspects of the god Osiris.

When archaeologists first began to explore the tombs of ancient Egypt in the 18th and 19th centuries, they found many hundreds of similar human-headed vases that were used to hold the preserved viscera of mummies. Through a simple misunderstanding, these came to be equated with the vases from Canopus and were called Canopic jars. This was an inappropriate designation, for they had nothing to do with that city or with Osiris.

Instead, they usually portrayed the deceased—or, in later times, the gods that presided over the mummification process.

In contrast, the find in Alexandria is the genuine article, depicting a young priest bearing a divine image, as a priest may have done in a procession or ritual ceremony over two thousand years ago.

Left: **Broken off at the ankles, this rare granite statue of a priest bearing Osiris-Canopus is over five feet tall. The young priest's hands are concealed beneath his cloak, illustrating, perhaps, that the effigy he is holding is too sacred to be touched with bare hands.**

Divers also found two sphinxes near the statue. Each about five feet long, they follow the Egyptian convention of having human heads. Well-preserved, they have even retained their noses—remarkable, since such protrusions are often destroyed by the wear and tear of time. Following a careful study of the sphinxes, Professor Zsolt Kiss of the Research Center for Mediterranean Archaeology at the Polish Academy of Sciences in Warsaw, Poland, determined their faces were those of late Ptolemies, one of them most likely Cleopatra's own father, Ptolemy XII. The presence of these sphinxes, and two others found at separate sites, strongly implies the one-time existence of religious installations in the area. And although they were sculpted separately and represent different rulers, this pair may have been part of the same religious edifice that contained the priest statue.

Still more artifacts on Antirhodos awaited discovery. In the small harbor of its southern extension a portion of a white-marble statue, once standing over six feet tall, was found, now broken off at the shoulder and missing part of one leg. According to Professor Kiss, this statue represents either the Greek god Hermes or a Ptolemaic king in the form of the god. Determining the sculptural style, whether Roman or Greek, has been difficult because the surface was badly deteriorated.

Perhaps the most surprising artifact to be uncovered was not a piece of statuary at all, but the extremely well preserved remains of an ancient shipwreck buried in the small harbor. Calibrated carbon-14 dating originally placed the wood between 90 B.C. and A.D. 130. Based on preliminary studies to date, it is believed that the wreck may be a Graeco-Roman or Roman cargo vessel or warship. Pieces of jewelry, amphorae, and food and bone remains were found nearby.

As the team wended its way up the ancient coastline, it encountered more intriguing artifacts. Most impressive was a twenty-seven-inch-high granite falcon head, which according to studies by Professor Jean Yoyotte, is a representation of the god Horus, son of

Philippe Rousseau, Alain Denaix, and Jean-Paul Blancan carefully secure the priest statue for raising. Most representations of Osiris-Canopus date from the beginning of Roman rule to the 2nd century A.D. Their presence in the Royal Quarter suggests that related cult buildings or temples were sited within the palace complex.

Isis. Efforts to date this well-crafted fragment continue. The horizontal fall of its wig piece suggests that it may have once come to rest on the back of an outstretched body. Based on his study of the head, Yoyotte has determined that it was once part of a monumental hawk-headed (or hieracocephalous) sphinx, the body of which was either that of a lion or a crocodile.

East of the Horus head, divers found an imposing granite head of a pharaoh bearing a royal headdress. After comparing such details as the fringed hair along its forehead and temples with relevant museum pieces, Professor Kiss identified it as being that of Octavian, Cleopatra's nemesis. Based on the size of the head, the statue from which it came was originally over sixteen feet tall.

Discovered north of the Octavian head was the fragment of a pedestal of excellent quality from pharaonic times, which features part of a foot of what was once a huge statue. Professor Yoyotte identified the hieroglyphic inscriptions on the base as referring to the pharaoh Merneptah, who ruled in the thirteenth century B.C. A third large but severely damaged sphinx lay near the base and a fourth sphinx, also badly eroded, was discovered on the main promontory of the peninsula.

Near the site, divers also found several other statues, including a white-marble head believed to depict Antonia Minor, daughter of Mark Antony. Northeast of the peninsula base along the ancient coast was a rare gray-granite sculpture fragment of a coiled serpent thought to be connected to Agathodaïmon, a god whose name is a Greek term signifying the "Good Spirit." Agathodaïmon is mentioned in ancient sources as the guarantor of prosperity of both Alexandria and its inhabitants. Near the serpent statue the team also discovered a limestone, headless statue of an ibis, the popular form of the god Thoth-Hermes, a combination god of wisdom, knowledge, writing, mathematics, and the reckoning of time.

Divers, archaeologists, and cameramen look on expectantly as the statue of a priest of Isis, one of the team's most prized discoveries, emerges into the modern world. Other works of similar quality may remain to be found, for the task of exploring the submerged city has just begun.

However marvelous were all of these individual relics, the team's principal task remained the recreation of ancient Alexandria. Much of the divers' time was spent on careful measurement, determining inch by inch the dimensions of dikes, paved courts, roadways—the enduring substructure of the city. The result of their labors was a detailed plan of its layout that clearly showed three separate harbors, all protected by elaborate breakwaters. The easternmost harbor lay in the lee of Cape Lochias and was no doubt the private royal haven mentioned by Strabo. A more open anchorage stood close by, protected from the swell by a man-made breakwater and three large reefs that must have made inshore navigation hazardous. To the west, Antirhodos formed the northwestern side of a parallelogram of sheltered water confined between the island, the Poseidium promontory, and the shore.

As the data mounted and the pieces of the jigsaw puzzle fell into place, Goddio and his colleagues realized that previous notions of ancient Alexandria's topography were substantially in error. Lacking any clear direction from Strabo, Mahmoud Bey had placed Antirhodos to the east of the Poseidium, while it in fact lay to its west. He had also depicted Cape Lochias as a small promontory only two or three hundred yards long, while it actually reached out like a giant lobster's claw almost three-quarters of a mile into the bay. Franck Goddio's remapping of the ancient topography will now serve as the accurate reference for all future studies of the area.

A diver shines his light on a red-granite block found on Antirhodos bearing the cartouche of Pharaoh Apries, a 6th-century ruler belonging to the 26th Dynasty.

Goddio's work may have caused the old maps to be rolled up, but much still remains to be done. Antirhodos, especially, is still an enigma. Its anarchic mixture of Roman, Greek, and pharaonic artifacts as well as the chaotic stone deposits and structural materials raise many questions regarding the city's social and architectural history. The recreation of Cleopatra's Alexandria is an ongoing task; the questions raised by the recent discoveries, says Goddio, will keep scholars busy for fifty years. He and his project codirector, Ibrahim Darwish, hope to continue the IEASM work on the site into the foreseeable future. As things stand, the very incompleteness of the findings only serves to stimulate the imagination.

Did world-weary Ptolemies plot and scheme on the sunken esplanades recently discovered off the present-day seafront? Is the barnacle-encrusted pavement bordering the main mouth of the western harbor the place where battle-scarred Antony retired to bemoan a world he lost for love? Most tantalizing of all, did Cleopatra's palace adorn the central esplanade of Antirhodos, and did the queen herself pace its columned halls, planning desperate stratagems as her fate was played out in faraway Rome? The port still holds secrets, and much remains to be discovered before the city the doomed queen loved finally reveals all its mysteries now hidden underneath the waves.

Taking Impressions Under Water

To permit scholars on land to study details of objects left underwater, Goddio and his team used a molding technique that sometimes improved on the originals it copied. While large objects such as statues were sometimes raised temporarily to the surface to permit three-dimensional casts to be made, most of the copying was done underwater, in keeping with the team's intent of disturbing the site as little as possible.

To obtain a permanent record of hieroglyphs and other markings on stone, divers were provided with a sheet of synthetic material called Tergal, cut to match the size of the block on which the inscription appeared and coated with a special silicone-rubber molding formula, *top left*. Attached to the Tergal were grips in the shape of buckles. Divers would then apply the Tergal onto the cleaned surface they wished to mold. Lead weights were attached to the buckles and a custom-formed sheet of lead placed atop the molding material to ensure adequate pressure, *bottom left*.

After about sixteen hours—typically, the period from an afternoon dive to the time of the first immersion the next day—the weights were removed and the hardened rubber sheet pulled away. The result was a supple and highly resistant molding that offered an incredibly clear impression of inscription details, *right*. The process was so successful that the impression was often easier to read than the eroded original. The molding was then photographed inverted, ready for translation.

Above: Divers examine hieroglyphs on a silicone molding impression that was taken from two broken sections believed to have originally served as a single pillar or the upright of a door. Clearly seen in the center of the molding is a line dividing the two pieces, whose collective hieroglyphs refer to Pharaoh Apries of the 26th Dynasty (656–525 B.C). Interestingly, these blocks were found at separate sites, one on Antirhodos and the other on the ancient submerged coast.

Enduring Impressions of Ancient Art

In agreement with the Egyptian Supreme Council of Antiquities, Franck Goddio and his team ensured that artifacts found in their exploration would remain in the East Port until a decision can be made about the possible creation of an underwater museum at the site. Yet the significance of some of their finds was such that they were unwilling to leave them untouched on the seabed without establishing a precise visual record of their appearance that would permit future scholars to study them in detail.

The solution lay in temporarily removing some objects from their underwater sites to permit casting and then returning them to the seabed. The replication process was overseen by Georges Brocot, a French artist who specializes in molding techniques. His task was to produce casts accurate enough in their details to produce near-exact replicas of the artifacts.

Before the process could begin, the object to be molded—here, a priest statue—underwent a thorough cleaning to remove foreign materials, including centuries of non-organic build-up, or concretion. To protect the statue's surface from the liquid silicone, it was coated with a very thin layer of petroleum jelly. Next, Brocot divided the statue into workable halves using plasteline, a type of modeling clay. This done, the statue was ready for the liquid silicone.

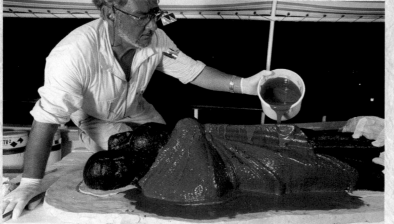

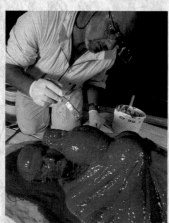

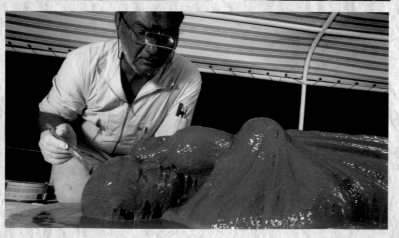

Left: **Wearing protective gloves and a magnifying attachment on his spectacles to permit detailed work, Brocot pours the molding material over the exposed front half of the statue. Using a small brush, he distributes the liquid evenly. Successive layers of silicone are added until the coating is at the desired thickness, about one-half inch (or half-centimeter). Once the material is set firm, Brocot applies gelcoat and a thick, epoxy-like resin to stabilize the mold shape.**

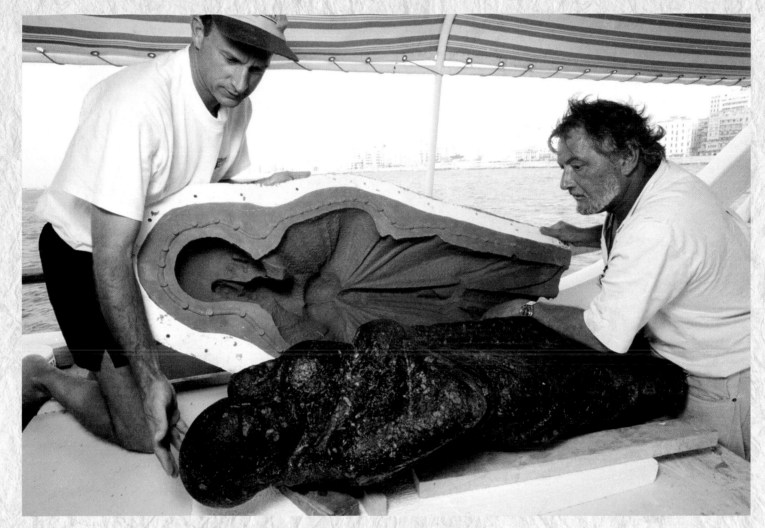

As Franck Goddio looks on, Georges Brocot removes a finished mold taken of the front half of the priest statue. The white material surrounding the hardened silicone is a thick resin applied at the end of the molding process that will help the mold retain its shape. Once the two mold halves are created, they are sealed together and used to create a perfect cast replica of the statue.

Diver Jean-Claude Roubaud
removes a mold from a
gigantic foot—part of what
remains of a monumental statue of
the pharaoh Merneptah. One of

more than ninety children of
Ramses II (Ramses the Great), this
New Kingdom ruler outlived twelve
elder brothers to succeed his
father on Ramses' death.

Right: Before it completely sets,
Georges Brocot performs final
detail work on the mold of the
statue head of Octavian.

The task of completing a thorough investigation of an expedition site often required the divers to temporarily displace large blocks and columns of stone to access the area underneath them. Here, Fernand Pereira carefully secures a granite block, which will be lifted a distance of a few yards using a system of inflatable airbags. Once excavation is complete, the stone is returned to its previously recorded position. *Right:* Roland Savoye examines a red-granite block for inscriptions.

Uncovering an Ancient Vessel

When divers first encountered pieces of timber jutting out from the seabed in the harbor of Antirhodos Island, they thought they may have stumbled on the remains of a jetty. The wood was extremely well-preserved, indicating the likelihood that it would probably date later than many of the artifacts they had already found. But when calibrated carbon-14 tests came back with a date range of between 90 B.C. and A.D. 130—a span including the lifetime of Cleopatra VII—excitement began to mount and Goddio ordered the site excavated.

Using water dredges to displace massive amounts of sediment, divers painstakingly uncovered what appeared to be the hull of an ancient ship. At the site they also found numerous amphorae, food and animal bone remains, and intriguing personal adornments such as rings and hairpins. The ship, over one-hundred-feet long and twenty-five-feet wide, was not to be disrupted, so Patrice Sandrin, a specialist in naval-architecture drawing, rendered each plank inch by inch onto waterproof synthetic paper, using a plastic lead pencil. Dive after countless dive, he recorded his findings onto an ever-growing master plan of the ship kept aboard the *Oceanex*. As the drawing took shape, another surprise was revealed—an apparent hole in the ship's keel, indicating that the vessel had been wrecked.

Several preliminary analyses of the wreck, which include comparative studies against similar known shipwrecks, point toward the possibility that this wreck is either a Graeco-Roman or Roman cargo vessel or warship.

Many questions remain to be answered about the vessel, including why it sank. Although there are dangerous reefs nearby, the damage to the keel is so extensive that it seems unlikely the ship could have got as far as the harbor before sinking if it had struck one. Yet the alternative possibility—that the ship was somehow rammed in the place where it went down—also raises many problems. While work on the vessel continues, it is still too soon to know whether the mystery of its final moments will ever be fully explained.

Left: This amphora, dating between the 3rd and 4th centuries A.D., although not associated with the wreck, was found at the site.

Right: Patrice Sandrin, a specialist in naval-architecture drawing, painstakingly records the details of the ancient ship's planks, shown below.

Far right: This wooden planking once lined the ship's hold.

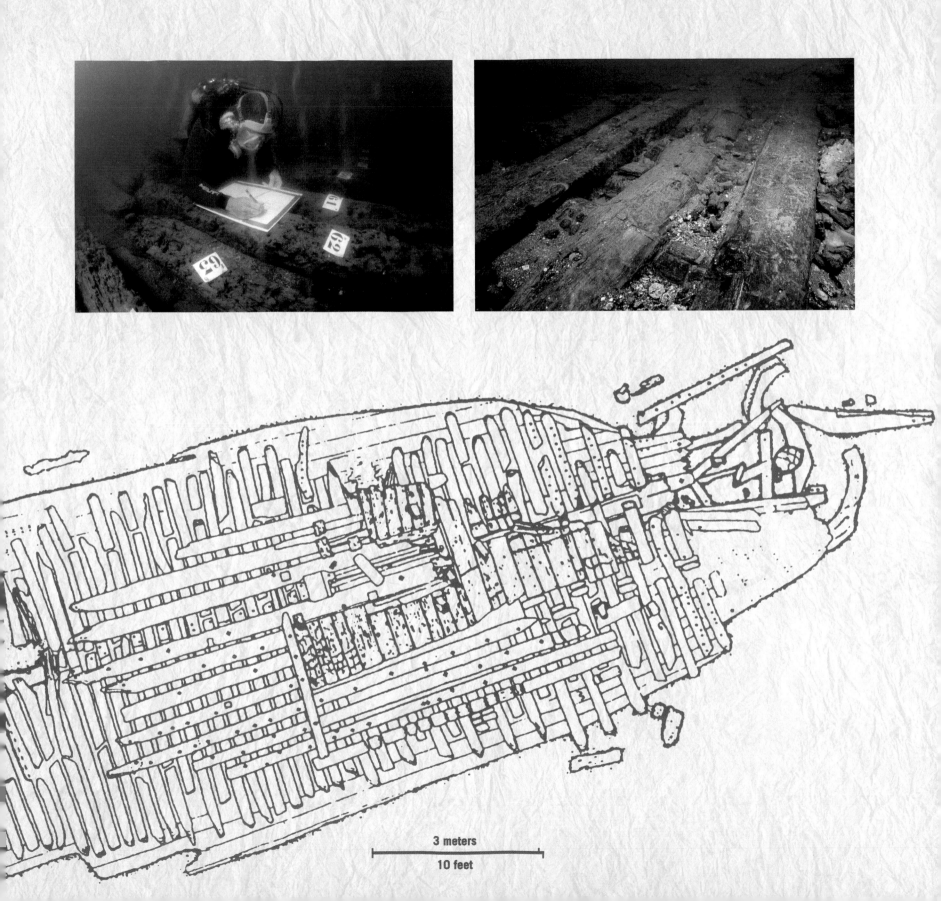

3 meters

10 feet

*B*elow . . . lies the harbour
that was dug by the hand
of man and is hidden from
view, the private property of
the kings, as also Antirrhodos,
an isle lying off the artificial
harbour, which has both a

royal palace and a small harbour.
—Strabo, *Geography*
Above: This detail taken from the
shipwreck that was uncovered
in the royal harbor of Antirhodos
shows a remarkably good state
of preservation.

Right: This basalt sphinx, one
of four discovered by Goddio's
team, was found along the ancient
shoreline. Although the face is
nearly indistinguishable, vestiges
of a royal headdress can still
be seen.

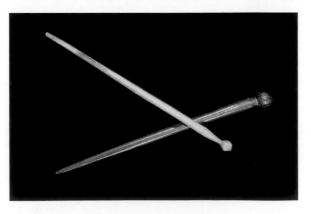

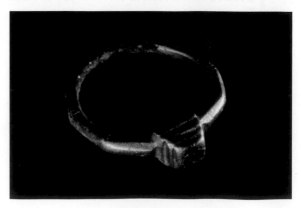

Goddio's team recovered a number of intriguing items near or within the site of the ancient shipwreck. Bronze nails, like the two shown opposite, *top,* were used in the ship's internal construction, away from contact with water. Other finds included a pair of hairpins, one of ivory and the other of ebony, *opposite, bottom left.* Most exciting of all were the two gold rings recovered. One, *right,* is set with an engraved chalcedony stone; the other, *opposite, bottom right,* bears a pyramidal decoration. Eating utensils, along with food remains that appear to be animal bones and hazelnuts were also retrieved, *above.*

This sphinx bearing the likeness of Ptolemy XII stares out into the murky waters of the East Harbor. Remarkably preserved, it may have once occupied the site of a temple on Antirhodos.

Previous spread: Patrice Sandrin records details of the ancient shipwreck timbers.

Following spread: Two sphinxes frame the priest of Osiris-Canopus.

GLOSSARY

Actium: A town on the coast of northwest Greece off which Octavian won a decisive sea battle over Antony and Cleopatra in 31 B.C. His victory cleared the way for his becoming Rome's first emperor.

Aegis: A representation of an Egyptian broad collar necklace that looks like a shield and was believed to protect the wearer with its magical power.

Alexandria: A Mediterranean seaport in Egypt, founded in 332 B.C. by Alexander the Great, and later the capital of the Ptolemaic dynasty. In ancient times, the trade and cultural hub of the Mediterranean world.

Amon: Divinity associated with that which is hidden from humanity. Amon was worshiped in Thebes as Amon-Re, king of the gods. In illustrations, this god usually wears a headdress with two long plumes or is shown as a ram, his sacred animal.

Ankh: A cross whose top arm is a loop. It symbolized eternal life in ancient Egypt.

Antirhodos: A small island in the Great Harbor of Alexandria.

Aphrodite: Greek goddess of love and beauty, analog of the Roman goddess Venus, sometimes associated with the Egyptian goddess, Isis.

Apis bull: A sacred bull associated with the Egyptian god Osiris. A succession of sacred bulls with distinctive markings were worshiped at Memphis.

Asp: A venomous, hooded serpent found in Egypt. The term is sometimes used to describe the viper.

Arsinoë IV: Younger sister and rival of Cleopatra VII.

Attic: Of, pertaining to, characteristic of Attica or Athens. Also the dialect of ancient Attica.

Auletes: Nickname meaning "flute player" for Ptolemy XII, father of Cleopatra VII.

Bacchus: Roman god of wine and revelry.

Barque: Sacred boat of the gods.

Berenice IV: Older sister of Cleopatra VII who ruled as Queen of Egypt 57–55 B.C.

Bas-relief: A sculpture in which the figures project slightly from the background.

Bes: The Egyptian patron deity of music, dancing, war, and childbirth, represented as a hairy dwarf having a tail and a lion's skin.

Book of the Dead: A collection of incantations and illustrations meant as a guide to the afterlife.

Brutus: Roman statesman and general and one of the conspirators who murdered Julius Caesar.

Byzantine: Pertains to the Byzantine Empire, A.D. 395–1453. Its capital was Byzantium, later Constantinople and then Istanbul. Also, pertains to the empire's art and architectural style.

Canopic Jars: Clay or stone jars used to hold a mummy's internal organs. Four jars decorated in the likenesses of Horus' sons (Imsety, Hapy, Duamutef, and Qebsenuef) held the stomach, lungs, intestines, and liver separately.

Caracalla: Roman emperor and military leader known for his brutal massacres of innocent people. His innovative reforms included granting Roman citizenship to all free inhabitants of the Empire.

Cartouche: An oval representing a rope ring, knotted at the base, inside of which is written the name of an Egyptian ruler. Meaning "cartridge" in French, the cartouche was so named by Napoleon's soldiers because its shape is similar to that of a bullet.

Charmion: A female servant and close companion of Cleopatra VII. She committed suicide along with her mistress.

Cicero: Roman orator and statesman, a champion of the Republic and avowed enemy of Antony and Cleopatra.

Cippus: A sacred Egyptian plaque. Waters poured over it were believed to have miraculous healing powers.

Dahebiah: A boat commonly used by tourists visiting Egypt in the nineteenth century.

Diadem: An ornamental headband worn by royalty.

Dionysus: Greek god of wine, mystical ecstasy, and immortality.

Drachma: An ancient Greek coin of silver or gold.

Dynasty: A line of rulers related by blood.

Electrum: An alloy of gold and silver, with gold predominating. This metal was used in Ancient Egypt to make jewelry, statues, and plating for obelisks.

Faience: A ceramic material made from crushed quartz and coated with a blue or green glaze. Used for jewelry as well as decorative and utilitarian objects.

Fulvia: Mark Antony's second Roman wife, who, with Antony's brother, led an unsuccessful uprising against Octavian in Italy. She died in Greece soon thereafter.

Gabinius: Governor of Syria and one of Pompey the Great's generals. He led the troops that restored Ptolemy XII Auletes to his throne after his exile.

Geb: Egyptian god of the earth and husband of the sky goddess, Nut.

Gladiator: In ancient Rome, a slave, captive, or paid performer who participated in the gladiatorial games. Gladiators fought animals or each other, usually to the death.

GPS: Global Positioning System. Technology developed by the U.S. government that uses satellites to determine latitude, longitude, altitude, and time anywhere on the planet.

Hathor: Egyptian goddess of love and joy. She was often depicted as a cow or as having cow's ears. She was believed to be the divine mother of the reigning pharaoh.

Hellenistic: Pertaining to the period of Greek culture bracketed by the death of Alexander the Great in 323 B.C. and the death of Cleopatra VII in 30 B.C.

Hercules: Greek and Roman hero and demigod legendary for his strength. Son of Zeus by Alcmena. The family of Mark Antony claimed descent from Hercules.

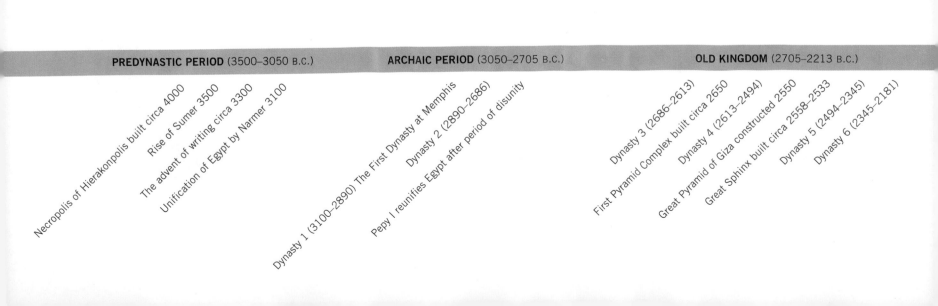

PREDYNASTIC PERIOD (3500–3050 B.C.)

ARCHAIC PERIOD (3050–2705 B.C.)

OLD KINGDOM (2705–2213 B.C.)

Necropolis of Hierakonpolis built circa 4000

Rise of Sumer 3500

The advent of writing circa 3300

Unification of Egypt by Narmer 3100

Dynasty 1 (3100–2890) The First Dynasty at Memphis

Dynasty 2 (2890–2686)

Pepy I reunifies Egypt after period of disunity

Dynasty 3 (2686–2613)

First Pyramid Complex built circa 2650

Dynasty 4 (2613–2494)

Great Pyramid of Giza constructed 2550

Great Sphinx built circa 2558–2533

Dynasty 5 (2494–2345)

Dynasty 6 (2345–2181)

GLOSSARY

Hieroglyphs: From Greek words meaning "sacred carvings," one of the three scripts used for writing in ancient Egypt.

Horus: Egyptian sky god, son of Isis and Osiris, often depicted as a falcon or with the head of a falcon. Pharaohs were considered his earthly embodiments.

Ibis: A small heron common along the Nile, sacred to the scribe god Thoth.

Iras: A female attendant and close companion of Cleopatra VII. She committed suicide with her mistress.

Isis: One of the most important and beloved deities in Egyptian mythology. She was a goddess of powerful magic and of wifely and maternal love, who, with her husband-brother Osiris, gave civilization to mankind.

Karnak: A temple in Upper Egypt sacred to the god Amon and other gods. It was the largest house of worship ever built.

Kheper or Khepri: A divine symbol for the rising sun, most often represented in the shape of a scarab beetle.

Kylix: A drinking cup in the shape of a shallow bowl with two horizontal handles and a footed stem.

Levant: The lands bordering the eastern shores of the Mediterranean; the Middle East.

Littoral: The seashore or coastal region that includes the land along the coast and the water near the coast.

Macedonia: An ancient kingdom in northern Greece, the native country of Alexander the Great.

Mammisi: A small temple on the main temple grounds, called a birth house, that celebrated the birth of the gods.

Modius: In Egyptian art, a cylindrical headdress often surrounded by cobra heads and topped with other symbols.

Muses: In Greek mythology, the nine goddesses of the arts and sciences.

Nemes: A cloth headdress worn by pharaohs; it adorns the head of the Great Sphinx at Giza.

Nile: A river in east Africa, flowing north 4,187 miles from its most remote headstream.

Nile delta: The area in northern (Lower) Egypt in which the Nile splits into five main branches that discharge into the Mediterranean Sea.

Nu pots: Containers for beer and wine.

Nut: Egyptian goddess of the sky, wife of the earth god Geb.

Obelisk: A tall, slender monument, usually a monolith, that tapers to a pyramidal top.

Octavia: Sister of Octavian, Roman wife of Mark Antony.

Osiris: Egyptian god of the dead, the husband-brother of Isis and father of Horus. The main centers of his cult were at Abydos and Philae.

Papyrus: An aquatic reed growing in the Nile. Its fibers were used to make paper for scrolls.

Pharaoh: A ruler of Ancient Egypt.

Philip II: King of Macedonia from 359 to 336 B.C.; father of Alexander the Great.

Plutarch: Greek biographer and historian whose collection of biographies is the original source of much of what is known today about the history of ancient Greece and Rome.

Ptah: An Egyptian creator god and patron of artisans, worshiped primarily at Memphis.

Ptolemy: The name of all the kings belonging to the Greek dynasty that ruled Egypt from 323–30 B.C.

Pompey the Great: Roman general and triumvir, defeated by Julius Caesar in Rome's second civil war.

Rhakotis: A village on the Mediterranean coast of Egypt founded as Alexandria by Alexander the Great.

Sarcophagus: An elaborately inscribed or ornamented stone casing for coffins.

Satrap: Provincial governor of the ancient Persian Empire.

Scarab: A dung beetle (Scarabaeus sacer) regarded in Egyptian mythology as a symbol of life because it seemed to generate spontaneously.

Scepter: A rod or wand carried as an emblem of regal or imperial power.

Sekhmet: Egyptian goddess of destruction. Sekhmet is usually depicted in the shape of a lioness or with the head of one.

Serapeum: Burial place of the sacred Apis bull.

Shem: A circular symbol representing eternal life in Egyptian mythology.

Sistrum: A musical instrument akin to a rattle, often used in religious ceremonies of ancient countries, including Egypt and Greece.

Sokar: An Egyptian god of cemeteries.

Sphinx: A lion with the head of a pharaoh, symbol of royal power.

Stela: An upright stone slab or pillar bearing commemorative inscriptions or designs.

Strabo: Greek geographer and historian who lived during the first centuries A.D. and B.C. and described the ancient city of Alexandria in his writings.

Sobek: Egyptian crocodile god.

Soter: Ptolemy I, founder of the Ptolemaic dynasty; name means "savior."

Timonium: The name Mark Antony gave to the seaside lodge he lived in briefly after his defeat at Actium.

Thoth: Ibis-headed god of writing.

Triumvirate: In ancient Rome, a coalition of three men who ruled jointly.

Was: A type of scepter, symbolic of power.

Zeus: King of the Greek gods, sometimes associated with Egyptian god Amon.

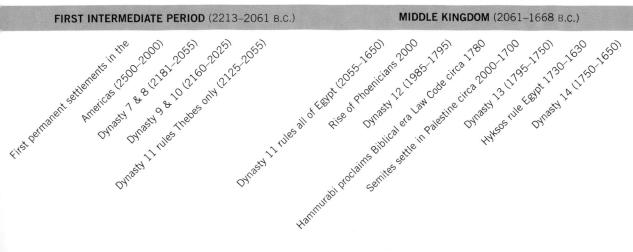

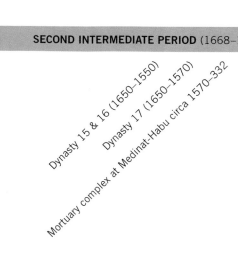

FIRST INTERMEDIATE PERIOD (2213–2061 B.C.) **MIDDLE KINGDOM** (2061–1668 B.C.) **SECOND INTERMEDIATE PERIOD** (1668–1570 B.C.)

First permanent settlements in the Americas (2500–2000)

Dynasty 7 & 8 (2181–2055)

Dynasty 9 & 10 (2160–2025)

Dynasty 11 rules Thebes only (2125–2055)

Dynasty 11 rules all of Egypt (2055–1650)

Rise of Phoenicians 2000

Dynasty 12 (1985–1795)

Hammurabi proclaims Biblical era Law Code circa 1780

Semites settle in Palestine circa 2000–1700

Dynasty 13 (1795–1750)

Hyksos rule Egypt 1730–1630

Dynasty 14 (1750–1650)

Dynasty 15 & 16 (1650–1550)

Dynasty 17 (1650–1570)

Mortuary complex at Medinat-Habu circa 1570–332

SUGGESTED READING

Aston, Mick, and Tim Taylor. *The Atlas of Archaeology*. London: DK Publishing, Inc., 1998.

Baines, John, and Jaromír Málek. *The Cultural Atlas of the World: Ancient Egypt*. Alexandria, Va.: Stonehenge Press, 1990.

Carradice, Ian. *Greek Coins*. First University of Texas Press. London: British Museum Press, 1995.

Cornell, Tim, and John Matthews. *Atlas of the Roman World*. Facts on File, Inc. Oxfordshire, England: Andromeda Ltd., 1982.

Davies, Vivian, and Renée Friedman. *Egypt Uncovered*. New York: Stewart, Tabori and Chang, 1998.

Delgado, James P., ed. *Encyclopedia of Underwater and Maritime Archaeology*. New Haven: Yale University Press, 1998.

Editors of Time-Life Books. *Empires Ascendant*. Alexandria, Va.: Time-Life Books, Inc., 1987.

———. *What Life Was Like on the Banks of the Nile*. Alexandria, Va.: Time-Life Books, Inc., 1997.

Flamarion, Edith. *Cleopatra: The Life and Death of a Pharaoh*. New York: Harry N. Abrams, Inc., 1997.

Foss, Michael. *The Search for Cleopatra*. Arcade Publishing, Inc. London: Michael O'Mara Books Ltd., 1997.

Forster, E. M. *Alexandria: A History and a Guide*. Garden City, N.Y.: Anchor Books, 1961.

George, Margaret, *The Memoirs of Cleopatra*. New York: St. Martin's Press, 1997.

Goddio, Franck, and André Bernand, Etienne Bernand, Ibrahim Darwish, Zsolt Kiss, Jean Yoyotte. *Alexandria: The Submerged Royal Quarters*. London: Periplus Ltd., 1998.

Gombrich, E. H. *The Story of Art*. 11th ed. London: Phaidon Press Ltd., 1967.

Gowing, Sir Lawrence, ed. *A History of Art*. Barnes & Noble Books. Oxfordshire, England: Andromeda Oxford Ltd., 1995.

Grant, Michael. *Cleopatra*. London: Weidenfeld and Nicolson, 1972.

Haas, Christopher. *Alexandria in Late Antiquity: Topography and Social Conflict*. Baltimore: The John Hopkins University Press, 1997.

Hayes, John W. *Handbook of Mediterranean Roman Pottery*. Published by special arrangement with the British Museum Press. Norman, Okla.: University of Oklahoma, 1997.

Hibbard, Howard. *The Metropolitan Museum of Art*. New York: Harrison House, 1986.

Janson, H. W. *History of Art*. New York: Harry N. Abrams, Inc., 1964.

Strabo's Geography: Book 17. Translated by Horace Leonard Jones and edited by G. P. Goold. Loeb Classical Library. Cambridge: Harvard University Press, 1996.

Ludwig, Emile. *Cleopatra: The Story of a Queen*. Translated by Bernard Miall. New York: The Viking Press, 1937.

The J. Paul Getty Museum. *Alexandria and Alexandrianism*. Malibu: The J. Paul Getty Museum, 1996.

Plutarch. *Lives*. Translated by Bernadotte Perrin. Loeb Classical Library. Cambridge, Mass.: Harvard University Press, 1914.

Renault, Mary. *The Nature of Alexander*. New York: Pantheon Books, 1975.

Romer, John. *Ancient Lives: Daily Life in Egypt of the Pharaohs*. New York: Holt, Rinehart and Winston, 1984.

Scholz, Piotr O., *Ancient Egypt: An Illustrated Historical Overview*. New York: Barron's Educational Series, Inc., 1997.

Siliotti, Alberto. *Guide to the Valley of the Kings*. Barnes & Noble Books. Vercelli, Italy: White Star S.r.l., 1996.

———. *Guide to the Pyramids of Egypt*. Barnes & Noble Books. Vercelli, Italy: White Star S.r.l., 1997.

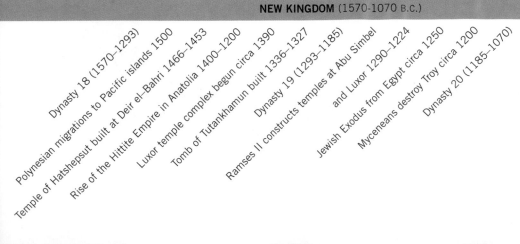

NEW KINGDOM (1570–1070 B.C.)　　　　**THIRD INTERMEDIATE PERIOD** (1069–747 B.C)

Dynasty 18 (1570–1293)

Polynesian migrations to Pacific islands 1500

Temple of Hatshepsut built at Deir el–Bahri 1466–1453

Rise of the Hittite Empire in Anatolia 1400–1200

Luxor temple complex begun circa 1390

Tomb of Tutankhamun built 1336–1327

Dynasty 19 (1293–1185)

Ramses II constructs temples at Abu Simbel and Luxor 1290–1224

Jewish Exodus from Egypt circa 1250

Myceneans destroy Troy circa 1200

Dynasty 20 (1185–1070)

Dynasty 21, 22, 23, & 24 (1070–767)

Kings at Tanis and Thebes rule 1069–747

Rise of Mayan culture in Mexico circa 900

Rise of Greek city-states circa 800

ACKNOWLEDGMENTS

The editors wish to thank the following individuals who helped in the development and production of this book: author and editor Laura Foreman, who brought Cleopatra to life; professor and Egyptologist Bob Brier of the C.W. Campus of Long Island University, who tirelessly shared his knowledge of the age; art historian Pat Remler, for her research on fine art and artifacts; Tony Allan and George Constable, whose editorial talents and expertise helped bring the story together; and Emily Teeter, Associate Curator at The Oriental Institute, The University of Chicago, who generously lent her time and expertise to the project. Thanks also to Michael Sedge, Carolyn Keating, Jeff Campbell, Ken DellaPenta, and Kate Pierce for their editorial contributions.

Final thanks go to all of the individuals who also contributed to the project: Tom Hastings, CineNova Productions, Toronto, Ontario, Canada; Sophie Lalbat, Salaction Public Relations, Paris; Tatiana Michel, Institut Europeén d' Archéologie Sous-Marine (IEASM); Georg F. Rosenbauer, Hilti Foundation, Liechtenstein; Mikol Rudd, Discovery Communications, Bethesda, Maryland; Gertraud Walch, Hilti Foundation, Liechtenstein; Sarah Wisseman, Director of the Department of Ancient Technologies, University of Illinois.

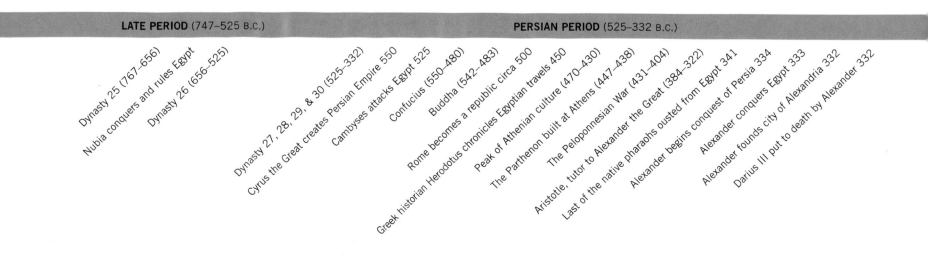

LATE PERIOD (747–525 B.C.)   **PERSIAN PERIOD** (525–332 B.C.)

Dynasty 25 (767–656)

Nubia conquers and rules Egypt

Dynasty 26 (656–525)

Dynasty 27, 28, 29, & 30 (525–332)

Cyrus the Great creates Persian Empire 550

Cambyses attacks Egypt 525

Confucius (550–480)

Buddha (542–483)

Rome becomes a republic circa 500

Greek historian Herodotus chronicles Egyptian travels 450

Peak of Athenian culture (470–430)

The Parthenon built at Athens (447–438)

The Peloponnesian War (431–404)

Aristotle, tutor to Alexander the Great (384–322)

Last of the native pharaohs ousted from Egypt 341

Alexander begins conquest of Persia 334

Alexander conquers Egypt 333

Alexander founds city of Alexandria 332

Darius III put to death by Alexander 332

IMAGE CREDITS

pp 2–3: © DCI, 1998. Photo by Jérome Delafosse.

pp 4–5: © DCI, 1998. Photo by Jérome Delafosse.

pp 6–7: © DCI, 1998. Photo by Jérome Delafosse.

pp 8–9: © DCI, 1998. Photo by Jérome Delafosse.

pp 10–11: © DCI, 1998. Photo by Jérome Delafosse.

pp 12–13: © Hilti Foundation/ UAD/Christoph Gerigk.

pp 14–15: Tom Wood collection.

p 17: Johannes Laurentius/ Antikenmuseum, Staatliche Museen. In the Bildarchiv Preussischer Kulturbesitz, Berlin.

pp 18–19: Giraudon/Art Resource, NY. "Cleopatra" by Alexandre Cabanel. In the Musee des Beaux-Arts, Beziers, France.

p 20: © Hilti Foundation/UAD/ Christoph Gerigk.

p 23: © DCI, 1998. Photo by Jérome Delafosse.

pp 24–25: © DCI, 1998. Photo by Jérome Delafosse.

p 26: Johannes Laurentius/ Antikenmuseum, Staatliche Museen. In the Bildarchiv Preussischer Kulturbesitz, Berlin.

p 28: Photo: AKG London/Cameraphoto. "Kleopatra lost die Perle auf" by Anton Schoonyans in 1706. In the Staatliches Kunstmuseum, Bukarest.

p 30: Bridgeman Art Library, London/New York. "Head of Alexander the Great" produced in the mid-second century. In the Architectural Museum, Istanbul, Turkey.

p 31: Bridgeman Art Library, London/New York. "Manuscript from History of Alexander the Great" by Louis Liedet. In the Bibliotheque Nationale, Paris, France.

p 32: Photo: AKG London. "Antique gold medallion with portrait of Philip II." In the Bibliotheque Nationale, Paris.

p 34: Bridgeman Art Library, London/New York. "L'Histoire du noble et valliant roy Alixandre le Grant" by a French artist in 1506. In the Bibliotheque Royale de Belgique, Brussels, Belgium.

p 36: Bridgeman Art Library London/New York/Philip Mould, Historical Portraits Ltd, London, UK. "Relief tablet of the Egyptian hieroglyphic titles of Alexander the Great" from the fourth century B.C.

p 37: Robert Harding Associates/George Rainbird Ltd. "Marble head of Ptolemy I Soter." In the Ny Carlsberg Glyptotek, Copenhagen.

pp 38–39: Illustration by Kevin Giontzeneli

p 40: Bridgeman Art Library, London/New York. "Eight drachma piece of Ptolemy I and Berenice" from the third century B.C. In the Hermitage, St. Petersburg, Russia.

p 41: Christie's Images. "Bronze figures of Isis, Horus, and Osiris."

p 42: Erich Lessing/Art Resource. "Detail of a wall painting in the tomb of Mennah" from the sixteenth to fourteenth century B.C. At an archaeological site, Luxor-Thebes, Egypt.

p 43: Christie's Images. "Pilgim flask and composition jar" from the third to first century B.C.

p 44: Bridgeman Art Library, London/New York. "Colored print of the Lighthouse erected by Ptolemy Soter on the Island of Pharos." In the O'Shea Gallery, London.

p 46: Christie's Images. "Bronze figure of a striding king" from the fourth to third century B.C.

p 47: © DCI, 1998. Photos by Jérome Delafosse.

p 48: Photo: AKG London. "Halle in der Alexandrinischen Bibliothek" from a book edited/written by H. Goell in 1876.

p 49: Bridgeman Art Library, London/New York. "Detail from a depiction of farming activities in the afterlife," 1250 B.C. In the British Museum, London.

p 50: © Photo RMN/H. Lewandowski.

p 51: The Stapleton Collection/Bridgeman Art Library, London/New York. "Plate 9 from Entwurf einer historischen Architektur," engraved by Johann Adam Delsenbach in 1721. In a private collection.

p 52: Werner Forman/Art Resource, New York. In Egyptian Museum, Cairo.

p 53: Christie's Images. "Winged scarab pectoral" from the fourth to third century B.C.; Christie's Images. "Egyptian new kingdom inlaid electrum ring" from 1550–1307 B.C.

p 54: Christie's Images. "Cleopatre essayente des poisons sur des condamnes a mort" by Alexandre Cabanel.

p 57: Photo: AKG London. "Cicero, in the Senate, accusing Catilina of conspiracy" by Cesare Maccari in 1889. In the Palazzo Madama, Rome.

p 58: Christie's Images. "Sandstone relief of a pharoah" from the second century B.C.

p 59: Christie's Images. "Limestone figure of a Ptolemaic queen" from the third century B.C.

p 60: Bridgeman Art Library, London/New York. "Gold bracelet." In the Egyptian National Museum, Cairo, Egypt; Bridgeman Art Library, London/New York. "Egyptian golden pectoral" from the fourth century B.C. In the State Russian Museum, St. Petersburg.

p 61: Christie's Images. "Alabaster cosmetic spoon" from the third to first century B.C.; Peter Willi/Bridgeman Art Library, London/New York. "Stela of Princess Nefertabet," 2600–2500 B.C. In the Musee des Beaux Arts, Grenoble, France.

p 62: © Hilti Foundation/UAD/ Christoph Gerigk.

p 63: © The British Museum.

p 64: Bridgeman Art Library, London/New York. "Kylix from Vulci: Flute Player and Dancer," made by Python, painted by Epiktetos in 520–510 B.C. In the British Museum, London.

p 65: Bridgeman Art Library, London/New York. "An Egyptian Feast" by Edwin Long in 1877. In the Bradford Art Galleries and Museums, West Yorkshire, United Kingdom.

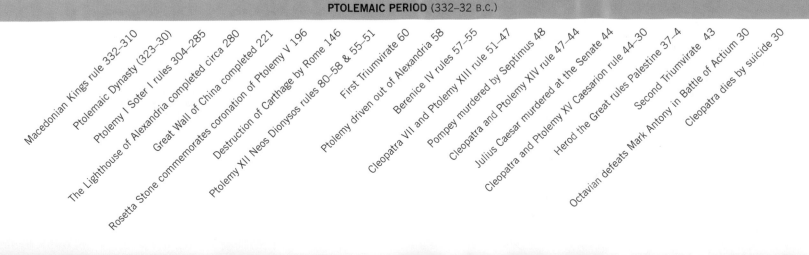

PTOLEMAIC PERIOD (332–32 B.C.)

Macedonian Kings rule 332–310

Ptolemaic Dynasty (323–30)

Ptolemy I Soter I rules 304–285

The Lighthouse of Alexandria completed circa 280

Great Wall of China completed 221

Rosetta Stone commemorates coronation of Ptolemy V 196

Destruction of Carthage by Rome 146

Ptolemy XII Neos Dionysos rules 80–58 & 55–51

First Triumvirate 60

Ptolemy driven out of Alexandria 58

Berenice IV rules 57–55

Cleopatra VII and Ptolemy XIII rule 51–47

Pompey murdered by Septimus 48

Cleopatra and Ptolemy XIV rule 47–44

Julius Caesar murdered at the Senate 44

Cleopatra and Ptolemy XV Caesarion rule 44–30

Herod the Great rules Palestine 37–4

Second Triumvirate 43

Octavian defeats Mark Antony in Battle of Actium 30

Cleopatra dies by suicide 30

Image Credits

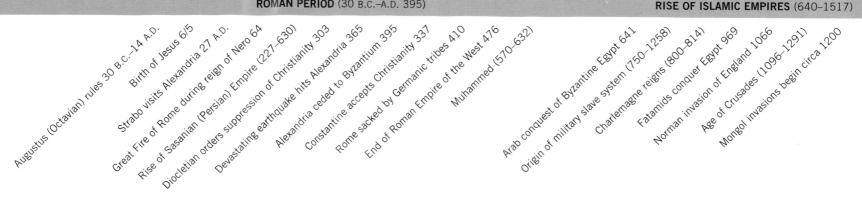

ROMAN PERIOD (30 B.C.–A.D. 395) **RISE OF ISLAMIC EMPIRES (640–1517)**

Augustus (Octavian) rules 30 B.C.–14 A.D.
Birth of Jesus 6/5
Strabo visits Alexandria 27 A.D.
Great Fire of Rome during reign of Nero 64
Rise of Sasanian (Persian) Empire (227–630)
Diocletian orders suppression of Christianity 303
Devastating earthquake hits Alexandria 365
Alexandria ceded to Byzantium 395
Constantine accepts Christianity 337
Rome sacked by Germanic tribes 410
End of Roman Empire of the West 476
Muhammed (570–632)
Arab conquest of Byzantine Egypt 641
Origin of military slave system (750–1258)
Charlemagne reigns (800–814)
Fatamids conquer Egypt 969
Norman invasion of England 1066
Age of Crusades (1096–1291)
Mongol invasions begin circa 1200

IMAGE CREDITS

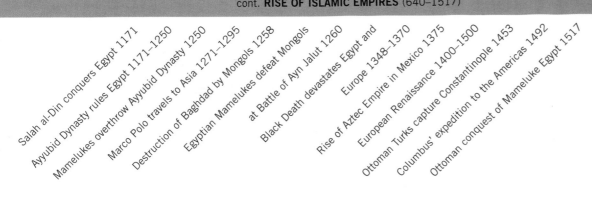

cont. **RISE OF ISLAMIC EMPIRES** (640–1517)

Salah al-Din conquers Egypt 1171
Ayyubid Dynasty rules Egypt 1171–1250
Mamelukes overthrow Ayyubid Dynasty 1250
Marco Polo travels to Asia 1271–1295
Destruction of Baghdad by Mongols 1258
Egyptian Mamelukes defeat Mongols at Battle of Ayn Jalut 1260
Black Death devastates Egypt and Europe 1348–1370
Rise of Aztec Empire in Mexico 1375
European Renaissance 1400–1500
Ottoman Turks capture Constantinople 1453
Columbus' expedition to the Americas 1492
Ottoman conquest of Mameluke Egypt 1517

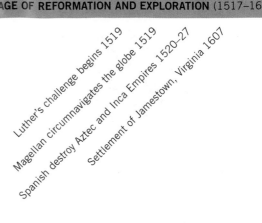

AGE OF REFORMATION AND EXPLORATION (1517–1620)

Luther's challenge begins 1519
Magellan circumnavigates the globe 1519
Spanish destroy Aztec and Inca Empires 1520–27
Settlement of Jamestown, Virginia 1607

INDEX

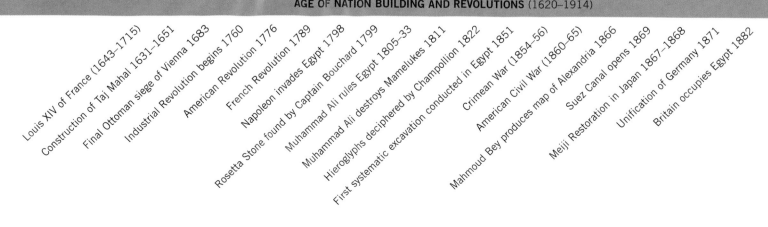

INDEX

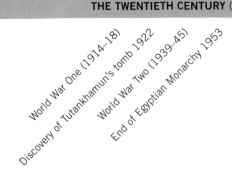

THE TWENTIETH CENTURY (1900–2000)

World War One (1914–18)
Discovery of Tutankhamun's tomb 1922
World War Two (1939–45)
End of Egyptian Monarchy 1953